MUSICALS

Rüdiger Bering

BARRON'S

Cover photos from top to bottom and left to right:
Audrey Hepburn in the film version of *My Fair Lady*, Warner Bros., Inc. / Minstrel Show, ca. 1840 / Liza Minelli in *The Act*, Time Inc./intertopics, © Martha Swope / Scene from *42nd Street*, Time Inc./intertopics, — Martha Swope / Anita Morris in *Nine*, Time Inc./intertopics, © Martha Swope / Scene from *Linie 1*, Grips Theater GmbH, Berlin / Scene from *Rent*, photo Joan Marcus / Fred Astaire and Cyd Charisse in the film version of *The Band Wagon*.
Back cover photos from top to bottom:
Poster for the film of *Brigadoon*, Heinz Bonn / Dance number from *Oklahoma!* / George Gershwin, Chappell/Intersong.
Frontispiece:
Scene from *42nd Street*, Time Inc./intertopics, Martha Swope.

American text version by: Editorial Office Sulzer-Reichel, Overath, Germany
Translated by: Anne Jeffers-Brown, Cambridge, Mass.
Edited by: Bessie Blum, Cambridge, Mass.

First edition for the United States and Canada
published by Barron's Educational Series, Inc., 1998.

First published in Germany in 1997 by
DuMont Buchverlag GmbH und Co. Kommanditgesellschaft, Köln, Germany.

Text copyright © 1997 DuMont Buchverlag GmbH und Co. Kommanditgesellschaft, Köln, Germany.

Copyright © 1998 U.S. language translation, Barron's Educational Series, Inc.

All inquiries should be addressed to:
Barron's Educational Series, Inc.
250 Wireless Boulevard
Hauppauge, New York 11788

Library of Congress Catalog Card No. 97-075289

ISBN 0-7641-0436-5

Printed in Italy by Editoriale Libraria

Contents

Preface

What makes a musical? Oscar Hammerstein II (who, interestingly, wrote not music but lyrics) had a very simple answer: "It can be anything it wants to be. There is only one thing a musical absolutely must have—music."

The truth is that in the one hundred or so years of its development, the musical has assumed so many different forms in so many different styles that an all-encompassing definition is nearly impossible. It is in fact no easy matter to differentiate between the musical and other genres. For one thing, there is no single style of music—styles range from the operatic characters in Kurt Weill's *Street Scene* through the operetta idiom of Frederick Loewe's *My Fair Lady* to the jazz-inspired sounds of Leonard Bernstein's *West Side Story* and the rock music in Galt MacDermot's *Hair*. Even the instrumentation varies from the classical orchestra to jazz ensembles and rock bands. In most musicals the songs arise out of the spoken dialogue, but there are also operatic-style scores, such as Andrew Lloyd Webber's *Evita*, where spoken dialogue is minimal.

Though the very designation "musical" is a shortened form of "musical comedy," the subjects and themes of musicals are as varied as their styles. From high tragedy to political satire to barely dressed up fluff, from *A Funny Thing Happened on the Way to the Forum* to *Cabaret* to *Miss Saigon*, a musical can be a musical play or a musical drama, as well as a comedy; it can tell a dramatic or even a tragic story, or hang some songs on a silly and superficial skeleton. Historical subjects find the same application as fairy tales; settings may be naturalistic, stylized, surreal, or satirical.

The musical is indisputably a product of the market-oriented system of private theater, sustained directly and solely by commercial success. Broadway, the undisputed center of the musical theater world, has always been a melange of the Old World and the New; European operetta has run side by side with jazz or vaudeville, in a tradition characterized by the melding of song, story, and dance, of tragedy and comedy, pathos and parody: The musical is the greatest distinctly American contribution to the world of theater.

This Crash Course outlines the development of the musical in terms of both art and business, informed by descriptions of prominent personalities and their individual contributions to the genre. In contrast to a more traditional musical guide, the focus is not on detailed plot descriptions, but on placing each work in a larger context. For further exploration of the subject, the book includes a bibliography, a selected discography, and a glossary.

Above all, however, it is hoped that this Crash Course will awaken interest in musical productions and inspire the reader's curiosity about pieces beyond classic and up-scale productions.

Rüdiger Bering

Old World, New World

The musical theater tradition of entertainment: drama—song—dance

Early forms of theater drew no distinct lines between song, drama, and dance; the differentiation between musical theater, drama, and ballet came much later. Indeed, the most popular forms of theater embraced song and dance alongside spoken dialogue. William Shakespeare (1564–1616) filled his comedies and romances—*Midsummer Night's Dream, Love's Labour's Lost, Much Ado About Nothing*—with song and dance, performed by "professional" entertainers such as clowns, troubadours, or fairies, or even by central characters themselves in masques and feasts. Many musical theater authors have cited Shakespeare's works as precursors of their own genre.

At the court of Louis XIV, the comic writer and dramatist Jean-Baptiste Poquelin, better known as Molière (1622–1673), worked with the composer Jean-Baptiste Lully to produce *comédie-ballets*—that is, ballet comedies—at the command of the dance and drama enthusiast Sun King. Together, the playwright and the composer produced pieces such as *The Bourgeois Gentleman*, which

integrated ballet and song with the action. In the "Avertissement" to his first *comédie-ballet*, *Les Fâcheux* (The Bores), Molière wrote: "Lest we interrupt the thread of this piece [by using musical interludes—ballets—between the acts of the comedy], we have tried our best to combine the subject of both the ballet and comedy into a single natural theme. Since this sort of combination is new in our theater, we might cite the authorities of antiquity as our precedent, and trust all will find this combination agreeable, and that it will serve as well as any other form to give us subject for reflection at our leisure."

The marriage of musical and dance interludes had to win public approval. Both Shakespeare

and Molière were theatrical producers as well as dramatists, and their success and survival were dependent on the vagaries of public taste as well as private patronage. We could not go so far as to claim that the plays of either Shakespeare or Molière constitute early musicals; they are simply dramas with music and dance interspersed as aesthetically, structurally, or thematically warranted. Shakespeare, Molière, and many of their respective contemporaries basically had no compunction about blending popular forms of theatrical production and entertainment.

The more direct ancestry of an ongoing musical theater begins in the 18th century with a popular debate over opera.

The Ballad Opera

Opera is a product of the Italian late Renaissance: In an effort to revive ancient Greek drama, the late 16th century composers Iacopo

Andrew Lloyd Webber's *Phantom of the Opera* is based on a novel by Gaston Leroux and derives its style from Romantic opera. Scene photo from the Hamburg production.

Stephen Sondheim's *Sunday in the Park with George* was inspired by the pointillist paintings of Georges Seurat. Scene photo from the original Broadway production.

Left:
William Shakespeare (1564–1616): Since 1938, when Richard Rodgers and Lorenz Hart reworked *The Comedy of Errors* into the musical comedy *The Boys from Syracuse*, Shakespeare's works have been used as the basis for many musicals: *Kiss Me, Kate* is based on *The Taming of the Shrew*; *West Side Story* sets the story of *Romeo and Juliet* in 1950s New York; and *Two Gentlemen of Verona* was an adaptation of Shakespeare's play by the same name. Shakespeare himself included song and dance in many of his plays and the use of music in many Shakespeare productions has ranged from the incidental to the central.

The first page of the score for John Gay and Johann C. Pepusch's *The Beggar's Opera*, for which Pepusch reworked popular ballads, folk songs, and dances.

The Beggar's Opera (satirical engraving by William Hogarth) became an early model for the entertaining musical theater. Like *The Threepenny Opera* by Bertolt Brecht and Kurt Weill, Duke Ellington based his jazz opera *Beggar's Holiday* (1946) on the work by Gay and Pepusch.

Peri and Giulio Caccini, together with the poet Ottavio Rinuccini, designated a new form, called "Dramma per musica." This somewhat formulaic construct of extended recitatives, short arias, duets, trios, and choral passages was elevated by Claudio Monteverdi into a new art form. The solo aria quickly became the dominant element of opera. Unfortunately, the accompanying trend toward combining vocal virtuosity with unrealistic subjects drawn from ancient mythology, with static action and stock characters, readily invited parody.

And parody came. On January 29, 1728, *The Beggar's Opera* was performed for the first time. Instead of ancient mythic heroes—the stuff that Restoration tragedy and epic poetry were made of—John Gay (1685–1732) and his musical collaborator Johann Christoph Pepusch brought criminals, whores, and beggars to the stage. Originally conceived as a satire on the *opera seria* of the time, *The Beggar's Opera* not only dealt the deathblow to the particular form it mocked, but also launched the tradition of the ballad opera. Instead of Belcanto and coloratura arias, it offered popular tavern songs and well-known melodies from works by Händel, Purcell, and other composers. The authors replaced sung recitatives with spoken dialogue and included dance numbers. The quarrel duet between Lucy and Polly over the crook Macheath parodied two Händel primadonnas who had descended into a hair-pulling brawl on a London stage. Like later musicals, *The Beggar's Opera* was a mixture of different elements that, in their skillful composition, formed an effective whole. After an unusually long run, the piece became a standard of the British theatrical canon

The success of *The Beggar's Opera*—which "made Gay rich and Rich gay" [John Rich was the manager of the Lincoln's Inn Fields Theatre where the satire was first mounted]—prompted Gay and Pepusch to write a sequel, *Polly*. However, in 1737, at the instigation of a humorless and insulted British Prime Minister Robert Walpole, Parliament banned satirical theater productions. The result was not only that *Polly* was not produced until 1777 (long after its author's death), but also that the development of the popular ballad opera as a form was considerably stalled. John Gay himself retreated into semi-retirement, writing texts for Georg Friederich Händel, whom he had previously satirized.

The New York premiere of *The Beggar's Opera* took place on December 3, 1750 in what was at the time still a British colony. *The Beggar's Opera* unleashed a wave of enthusiasm in New York, and laid the foundation for the tradition of American musical theater. Some of the songs had already found their way to North America, and in 1735, in Charleston, South Carolina, the ballad opera *Flora* was presented; *Flora* may well have been the first staged music production in what would later become the United States.

Wolfgang Amadeus Mozart's *The Magic Flute* was produced like a musical as a commercial production of Emanuel Schikaneder's People's Theater. The typical musical form, with two acts and a brief intermission, was already set. This historical color engraving shows the stage setting of the original production, Act I.

Singspiel, opera buffa, opéra comique
At the beginning of the 18th century a musical theater form emerged on the European continent. Unlike the *opera seria*, which was produced mostly in royal courts, the new genre had a more

1700 – 1918

From so-called *intermezzi*—comic one-acts that filled intermissions between the acts of serious operas—came the Italian *opera buffa*, a mid-18th century Italian comic opera.

Philosopher Jean-Jacques Rousseau established the *opéra comique* in Paris with *Le devin du village* (*The Village Soothsayer*).

popular sound and appeal. The enlightened German middle class demanded musical comedies in their own language; to satisfy this demand, a series of works were composed with parts in them for actors. In Vienna, where Emperor Joseph II in 1778 called for the composition of such musical comedies—albeit for educated singers—the form reached its peak with Wolfgang Amadeus Mozart's *The Abduction from the Seraglio* and *The Magic Flute*, written for the Vienna Folk Theater to a libretto by Emanuel Schikaneder. In Naples, from the beginning of the 18th century, the *commedia dell'arte* flourished. This Italian form of improvisational musical comedy was based on Neapolitan folk traditions. In the early 19th century, composers such as Rossini (*The Barber of Seville*) and Donizetti (*The Elixir of Love*) carried on the tradition of *opera buffa*. The *opéra comique*, which emerged at about the same time in France, dispensed with the Italian style of sung recitatives in favor of spoken dialogue. In time, the parodic and comical elements dropped away to the point where, near the end of the century, *opéra comique* could also treat tragic subjects, as in George Bizet's *Carmen*.

All these European forms of entertaining musical theater were rooted in the traditions of popular culture, and were chiefly produced at commercial theaters. This was also true of operetta, which emerged in the mid-19th century from comic opera, and would in time conquer not only Europe but also the New World.

The birth of operetta

Jacques Offenbach was born in 1819 in Cologne, the son of a Jewish choirmaster. By the age of six he had learned to play the violin, and in 1832 his father sent the musically gifted child to Paris, where Offenbach—although really still

The Birth of Operetta

too young—attended the conservatory. At fifteen, he was earning his living as a cellist in the orchestra of the *Opéra Comique*. Three years later he produced his first stage work, *L'Alcove*, an *opéra bouffe* in one act. The prospect of an international crowd for the Paris Exposition of 1855 prompted Offenbach to buy a theater near the Champs-Elysées; the theater seated exactly 50 and was originally limited by law to allow no more than three performers per production. On July 5, 1855, Offenbach opened the "Théâtre des Bouffes-Parisiens" with the one-act *Les deux aveugles* (*The Blind Beggars*), about two street musicians who fight over their alms. Encouraged by the success of this piece, Offenbach, now a seasoned theatrical producer, brought out more of these satirical short operas

Jacques Offenbach's Parisian operettas were the prototype for many later musicals.

called "Musiquettes" before he attempted a full-length work: On October 21, 1858, *Orphée aux Enfers* (*Orpheus in the Underworld*) opened at the Bouffes-Parisiens. And with this stroke

of genius Offenbach invented a new form of musical theater: the operetta. *Orpheus in the Underworld* unites an impudent operatic parody (primarily of Gluck's *Orpheus and Eurydice*) with biting political satire, popular couplets with refined ensemble numbers, cheerful melodies with the wild and provocative can-can. In further works, Offenbach varied his successful formula and caricatured Second Empire society. By the time of his death in 1880, Jacques Offenbach had created over 100 operettas of different lengths. His most ambitious opera, *The Tales of Hoffmann*, was only produced posthumously, so its author never enjoyed its triumph, though it still graces the standard international repertoire.

Offenbach's *The Blind Beggars* in a 1990 staging at the Semperoper in Dresden, Germany.

Original poster for *Orpheus in the Underworld*.

The dance craze sparked by Offenbach's can-can music from *Orpheus in the Underworld* even reached the wild west (here in an illustration from *The Adventures of Lucky Luke*).

Offenbach's operettas were produced all over Europe; in Vienna and London, his work inspired composers like Johann Strauss and Arthur Sullivan. By 1883, operetta fever, which had spread like an epidemic after the New York premiere of *La Vie Parisienne* (Parisian Life), reached an early peak.

With the witty and spirited French operetta, Offenbach had developed a basic formula for musical comedies, which would be used in later years by many a musical production. Seventy years after Offenbach's death, Cole Porter carried on the tradition of the mythic travesty with *Out of This World*, and his can-can celebrated the "Parisian Life."

In the original Vienna production of *Orpheus in the Underworld*, Austrian comedian and playwright Johann Nestroy played Jupiter—here appearing as a fly.

Operetta crosses the Atlantic

The Viennese operetta made its way across the Atlantic in the first decade of the 20th century, and its waltz rhythm conquered Broadway. Franz Léhar's *Merry Widow* renewed a wave of enthusiasm for imported European operettas that threatened to stifle any attempts at indigenous American musical theater. French and Viennese pieces still outpaced the popularity even of the English team of Gilbert and Sullivan.

Composer Arthur S. Sullivan began and established his career with more traditional endeavors in classical music—mostly hymns and music for royal pageantry that enjoyed a fair amount of popularity in their time, albeit eclipsed in time by others and by his own greater fame for operettas. In 1871 the impresario Richard D'Oyly Carte paired him up with author and humorist William Schwenck Gilbert to write operettas. Their first collaborative success was the one-act *Trial by Jury*, which they followed with thirteen full-length operettas. The first of these appeared in 1878: *HMS Pinafore*, a satire on the imperial navy, was produced first in Boston and then on Broadway to unprecedented acclaim. *Pinafore* played simultaneously at eight New York theaters, with nearly a hundred touring companies throughout North America. Unfortunately for the smash hit's authors, the countless productions brought them no royalties—the United States had made no international copyright agreements for the operetta. To prevent anything of the kind from happening with their next work, *The Pirates of Penzance*, on the day before its scheduled premiere in 1879 in New York, a reading of the new piece was given by the touring company of *Pinafore* in the little southern English town of Paignton before an audience of 45 (in order to secure rights in Europe).

Only a year after its premiere in 1909, Oscar Strauss's *Der tapfere Soldat* opened in New York as *The Chocolate Soldier*. The show was based on a play by George Bernard Shaw. Shaw, however, dissociated himself from the musical adaptation and vehemently opposed plans to turn his *Pygmalion* into a musical. *My Fair Lady* had to wait until after the playwright died.

The Pirates of Penzance

An orphan boy, Frederic, upon reaching the age of majority, completes his apprenticeship on a pirate ship (to which he had been bound in error, instead of to a "pilot"). Frederic's sense of honor kept him loyal to his pirate brethren as long as his

1700 – 1918

Pirates: Cards from packets of Players cigarettes.

apprenticeship bound him to them, despite his moral distaste for the life that they lived. He ventures ashore where he meets Mabel, the charming daughter of a Major General and wishes to marry the young woman. The "Very Model of a Modern Major General" and his daughters fall into the hands of the pirates, but he manipulates their sentimentality by telling them he, too, like all of them, is an orphan. Frederic, meanwhile, is recalled to pirate duty by an unfortunate twist of semantics: He was born on February 29 in a leap year, and, thus, although he is twenty-one years old, he has only celebrated five birthdays, and he must serve his apprenticeship until his twenty-first birthday, sixty years hence. The prospect of waiting for him saddens Mabel. The local constabulary are informed of the pirates' presence and their confrontation is resolved by a *deus ex machina* when Queen Victoria descends from above: As honorable citizens, the pirates bow to their queen. They then discover that they are all of noble lineage; thus, nothing stands in the way of their marrying the daughters of the Major General.

Gilbert and Sullivan, who supposedly could not stand each other and pursued their collaboration as much as possible by mail, were clearly influenced, both musically and thematically, by Jacques Offenbach. To Sullivan's musical mixture of English church anthems, French dance rhythms, and satirical operatic pathos, Gilbert wrote ironic texts marked by rapier wit, masterly nonsense, and elocutionary legerdemain. His verbal prowess was not easily translated, and Gilbert and Sullivan, understand-ably, met with greater success across the Atlantic than across the Channel.

American operetta

Influenced by the imported European works, more and more operettas began to appear in America as well. Among the most successful American composers of the first decade of the 20th century were Rudolf Friml, Gustav Lüders, Karl Hoschna, Ludwig Englander, and Gustav Kerker, all of them born in Germany or in the Austro-Hungarian monarchy. In fact, up until the United States' entry into World War I, a German-sounding name was something akin to a key to success for com-posers of light entertainment. Outrageously popular works in their own day, few have stood the test of time. Irish-

The Pirate King in a 1996 German performance at the Berlin Theater of the West.

man Victor Herbert, who was raised and re-ceived his musical education in Stuttgart, pre-ceded Gershwin and Bernstein in successfully crossing the borders between classical and popu-lar theater music. As director of the Pittsburgh Symphony Orchestra, Herbert had no qualms about composing entertaining music. He was also one of the founders of ASCAP, the union for com-posers, authors, and publishers. Herbert's works were often set in exotic countries such as Egypt, India, Afghanistan, or Persia. Four of his operet-tas were produced in the 1899/1900 season, each set in a different wine-making center.

Born in Hungary, Sigmund Romberg journeyed to New York and never returned to Europe.

Romberg got a job playing at a piano bar, where his own songs piqued the interest of the powerful theater owner J. J. Shubert. Shubert commissioned Romberg to compose some pretty melodies for stage productions, with explicit instructions that the music must under no circumstances divert attention from the focus of the show—the chorus girls. Advertisements for the production never even mentioned the composer's name, but Shubert's patronage did mark the beginning of a remarkable career. Between 1914 and 1917 alone— in a mere 26 months— Romberg wrote stage music for 14 productions (revues, operettas, and musical comedies), for which he often reworked pieces by European composers. His biggest successes were *Maytime* (1917), based on a Berlin operetta by Walter Kollo, *Blossom Time* (1921), based on a Viennese *singspiel*, and *The Student Prince in Heidelberg* (1924). The latter was a nostalgic work, still occasionally staged, about the star-crossed love between a prince and a barmaid. In all his works produced in New York, even *Up in Central Park* (1945), Romberg remained faithful to the bittersweet world of 19th-century operetta. Unlike the music of other early American operetta composers, some of Romberg's melodies, such as "Lover Come Back," recorded by the great jazz and blues singer Billie Holiday, have endured.

Victor Herbert's great success was the operetta *The Red Mill*, set in Holland. The 1906 production marked the first time electric stage lighting was used on Broadway.

Prince and barmaid: *The Student Prince* by Sigmund Romberg.

Rise of the American Theater

Entertainment, not literature

Up to the mid-19th century, the American theater was dominated by European influences; efforts to establish an independent American idiom could hardly find recognition. In the late 17th century, when English touring troupes visited the North American colonies, the Puritan population greeted them with barely concealed hostility. The first reference to a stage production in the New World is in a 1665 court judgment from Virginia: Three men were decried by villagers for producing a theater piece written by one of the three. The judge absolved them of any wrongdoing.

In the early 18th century, the mostly English theatrical troupes supported a regular theater industry and listed new pieces like *The Beggar's Opera* alongside classic Shakespearean fare. In the 19th century, theatrical families like the Barrymores and the Hammersteins first stepped onto the landscape of the American stage, where they would remain for several generations; and, the American theater produced world-class performers such as Edwin Booth. Still, efforts to forge a literary theater on the European model foundered for want of important dramatists and a wide audience.

Assassination in the theater: John Wilkes Booth, a character actor well known in his time as a member of a theatrical family, is known today as the man who killed President Lincoln. The Confederate partisan shot Lincoln at the Washington Opera House in 1865. His character appears in Stephen Sondheim's 1987 musical *Assassins*.

During the 19th century, the cities of the New World grew astronomically in the face of the industrial revolution and continual waves of immigration. This demographic explosion resulted in an entirely new urban life-style among the multi-class, multi-ethnic populations. One manifestation of such change was a growing demand from the working and middle classes for entertainment–for popular amusements. And this demand was heard, loud and clear.

The voice of the city

The notorious Bowery on the Lower East Side of Manhattan–now more famous for Bowery bums, the forerunners of today's urban homeless–was once the largest entertainment district in New York. There, concert saloons or honky tonks, known as vaudeville palaces, opened up next door to brothels and gambling dens. These theaters sprang up with as much diversity as the population itself: Since most immigrants had a limited command of English and many had little or no education, anyone who wanted to appeal to a variety of audiences was essentially obliged to avoid highly verbal productions. Burlesque shows, made up of assorted numbers with no particular cohesive theme, were offered in an atmosphere reeking of rotgut and smoke. Sentimental songs about unfulfilled love and the longing for a distant home alternated with bawdy humor and drastic satire, as well as spectacular acts by sword swallowers and jugglers. Like the public, the vaudevillians reflected New York's so-called melting pot: Italian prima donnas appeared alongside Yiddish and Irish comedians, and African-American singers and tap dancers.

Like other forms of entertainment, vaudeville was also a business—"Show Business." Theater entrepreneur Tony Pastor seized an opportunity to elevate vaudeville out of its disreputable environment and to transform it into entertainment suitable for the whole family. Previously, the vaudeville audience had been almost all men (or not very proper women). When Pastor opened his theater on Broadway in 1861, to make the environment more appealing to decent families, he prohibited smoking and drinking during the show; later he

The designation "vaudeville" is a corruption of the French "voix de ville"— voice of the village.

handed out coupons and vouchers for household articles or toys to the women and children. The idea was a hit: Vaudeville was transformed into popular entertainment for the middle class (leaving "burlesque" in the smoke and dust). Touring companies brought the popular shows to the whole country. Almost all of the important

This 19th-century audience expresses its opinion of a performance very clearly: the entertaining theater must cater to public taste.

Silent movie comedian Buster Keaton (right) began his career in vaudeville at the age of three in an act with his parents. His artistic ability and famous deadpan style were apparent at an early age.

American performers and comedians of the first half of the 20th century—among them, escape artist Harry Houdini and film comedians such as the Marx Brothers—began their careers in vaudeville.

By the middle of the 20th century, with live theater increasingly supplanted by radio, movies, and television, the vaudeville tradition slowly and steadily declined. Not only audiences, but performers, producers, directors, but writers as well, were wooed away by the prospects of the newer media.

Burlesque

Originally, a burlesque was a travesty of famous dramas (or sacred cows) such as Shakespeare's *Hamlet*; the burlesque's central characters spoofed and parodied such serious actors as Edwin Booth. In the path of this satirical maelstrom, public personalities and current events also came in for a lambasting. But at the center of the burlesque were always song and dance. In 1868, the "British Blondes," an English troop of blond dancers led by Lydia Thompson, came to Broadway as guest stars. The British Blondes offered a crude mixture of dances, songs, and an inchoate act loosely based on Greek mythology. The erotic appeal of the scantily clad performers caused a public sensation. Before long, burlesque was synonymous with bare legs and striptease shows. Once utterly scandalous, burlesque reached a certain glamorous peak in the 1930s with the legendary stripper Gypsy Rose Lee, whose 1959 autobiography became the basis of the musical *Gypsy*, which in itself paints a vivid backstage picture of the vaudeville and burlesque life.

The triumph of spectacle

Two years before the British Blonds, a French dance company appeared in one of the most spectacular theatrical productions of the 19th century. In 1866, two American producers, Henry C. Jarrett and Harry Palmer, saw a ballet show in Paris called *La Biche du Bois*; they signed thirty-five of the ballet's dancers for a guest performance on Broadway. Before the dancers made it to New York, however, the Academy of Music, the planned venue, burned down. At the same time, the manager of Niblo's Garden, one of New York's largest theaters, was having doubts about whether a melodrama by Charles M. Barras signed for his venue would be a success. The dark play, *The Black Crook*, combined the pact-with-the-devil themes of two famous operas, *Der Freischütz* by Carl Maria von Weber and Gounod's *Faust*.

The Burlesque *Pocahontas* by Irish comedian John Brougham was produced in the gigantic Bowery Theater.

Jarret and Palmer, in their search for a new theater, devised a plan to include the French dancers along with a few current popular hits with the scheduled melodrama. Although it lasted five and a half hours, *The Black Crook* was a smashing success. It ran in New York for 16 months, toured to enthusiastic houses across the country, and was repeatedly revived through the 1920s. The show earned approximately a million dollars. The reaction of the New York press was a mixture of praise and disgust. The reviewer for the *New York Tribune* wrote: "The production is grand, the ballet very beautiful, the play is—manure." Any other drama, he suggested, would have served just as well as a pretext for showing off women's legs. Nonetheless, critics praised the splendor of the scenery, the theater

NIBLO'S GARDEN

LESSEE AND MANAGER .... WM. WHEATLEY.
STAGE MANAGER .... L. J. VINCENT.

Doors open at Seven.   Curtain rises quarter before Eight.

September 12, 1866.—First Night.

EVERY EVENING

AND

SATURDAY AFTERNOON

AT TWO,

Will be presented, after a preparation of several months, and

AN ACTUAL OUTLAY OF OVER

FIFTY THOUSAND DOLLARS

The Original, Grand, Romantic, Magical and Spectacular Drama in Four
Acts, by CHAS. M. BARRAS, Esq., entitled The

BLACK CROOK

The sole right of which production in New York and its vicinity
has been purchased by Mr. WHEATLEY; who has also entered into an agreement with

MESSRS. JARRETT & PALMER

For the introduction of their Great

PARISIENNE BALLET TROUPE,

Under the direction of the renowned Maître de Ballet

SIGNOR DAVID COSTA,

(Of the Grand Opera, Paris,) who will appear in a

MOST COSTLY AND MAGNIFICENT DRAMATIC SPECTACLE

EVER PRESENTED IN AMERICA

The original poster for *The Black Crook*.

1700 – 1918

Four attractive French dancers celebrated by New York audiences in *The Black Crook*.

technology, the walls of mist in which silvery coaches, filled with lolling lascivious fairies, swung through the air. While *The Black Crook* was not a musical as we think of musicals today—dramatic scenes, songs, and dances followed one another abruptly—the triumph of the spectacle set a standard still perceptible in today's mammoth productions, where helicopters land onstage or the theater itself may be transformed into a roller-skating rink.

Behind the scenes of *The Black Crook*: The dancers prepare for their entrance in the "air ballet." Flying machinery was one of many special technical effects.

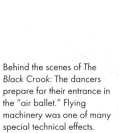

The success of *The Black Crook* spawned more and more costly "extravaganzas" in its image. The Hippodrome, built in 1905 to hold 5,200 spectators, with a 115-foot-deep stage, complete with a filled pond, served as the backdrop for many such spectacles. Among the most popular subjects were the utopian novels of Jules Verne.

In 1946, Orson Welles wrote and produced a show based on Verne's *Around the World in 80 Days*, with music composed by Cole Porter.

In this instance, however, Welles missed the mark—the heyday of these extravaganzas was past; the Hippodrome had been demolished in 1936, and the production was a commercial flop.

Minstrel shows

Around 1800, an immigrant comedian named Johann Gottlieb Graupner blackened his face with burnt cork and appeared under the stage name "The Gay Negro Boy," singing and playing the banjo. Other white actors followed his example, and the racist stereotype of the shiftless, happy-go-lucky Negro became a familiar figure on touring stages. Thomas D. Rice staged entire productions centered on his stage persona "Jim Crow." He called them "Ethiopian Operas." In 1843 a composer named Dan Emmett appeared in blackface with

three colleagues; the quartet called themselves the "Virginia Minstrels." Each played an instrument (tambourine, banjo, violin, and the castagnettes, called Bones); they imitated the songs, dances, and diction of slaves in the American South. The typical formula of the minstrel show included solo and group songs, instrumental musical numbers, dances and parodies, and dialogues between the

A minstrel show, ca. 1840. The performers on the left and right were called "Mr. Bones" and "Mr. Tambo" respectively, for the purposes of comic dialogue.

The revue star Al Jolson, who showed his own face in the first sound movie *The Jazz Singer* (1927), began his career as a minstrel performer in blackface.

whitefaced Mr. Interlocutor—a kind of master of ceremonies who sat in the middle—and the endmen (also called "cornermen"), named for their instruments, Mr. Tambo and Mr. Bones, who sat around him. A minstrel show always ended with a hoedown, a wild dance of the whole ensemble.

After Abraham Lincoln abolished slavery in 1863, many black performers also appeared as minstrels, but this first distinctly American form of entertainment really remained the province of white men. Women did not generally participate. Certainly, blackface today is considered unthinkably racist, as it was in the past—even if more accepted by a generally insensitive public. Paradoxically, certain African-American elements like tap dancing managed to make their way from the minstrel shows into popular culture, and in time attained a certain degree of respect. Dan Emmett, whose song "Dixie" became known as the anthem of the southern states, and Stephen Foster, composer of popular melodies such as "Oh, Susanna" and "My Old Kentucky Home," included authentic black American sounds in their songs for the minstrel stage. The popularity of the minstrel shows peaked between 1870 and 1880, and then very quickly waned.

Yankee Doodle Dandy

At the turn of the century almost all the elements that make up the musical were in place: Beside the form and dramaturgy of the European operetta, Broadway flourished as an ongoing theater business, with a tradition of maintaining stage art, the necessary singers, dancers, and actors, and an entertainment-hungry public.

1700 – 1918

The inclusion of black folklore in minstrel shows pointed the way to an independent musical language. The 1874 extravaganza *Evangeline* was the first to be designated a "musical comedy." In the first years of the new century, however, Broadway was still dominated by European operettas and American imitations.

Into the heart of this European dominance stepped George M. Cohan. Like Victor Herbert before him, he was of Irish descent, but unlike the academically trained Herbert, Cohan was a purely self-taught man and came from the completely different traditions of vaudeville and the minstrel show. As the son of show people, Cohan spent his childhood touring the vaudeville circuit throughout the United States with his parents and sister. "The Four Cohans" became one of the best-known acts in vaudeville.

George M. Cohan contributed to that fame in every way: Not only did he write all the songs and lyrics, he also took over the role of manager. His

George M. Cohan (right), with his parents and sister, trod the boards in vaudeville as *The Four Cohans*.

great goal, like that of many a vaudeville legend, was to reach the theater mecca of New York City. On February 25, 1901, the curtain went up for the first time on a Broadway musical written and produced by George M. Cohan. *The Governor's Son*, alas, did not bring the hoped-for success, and, to top it off, in the first scene Cohan injured his ankle so badly that he had to hobble around the stage for the rest of the show. Cohan did not give up, however, and three years later, with *Little Johnny Jones*, he mounted the first in a remarkable series of hits. In his role as impresario, he served himself as composer, lyricist, author, director, and star. His pieces glorified himself, his family, and—America. In the hit song "Yankee Doodle Dandy," he styled himself as "a real live nephew of my Uncle Sam, born on the Fourth of July." Well, nearly: Cohan's birth certificate in fact gives his date of birth as July 3, 1879. He praised the grand old American flag, wrote the stirring march "Over There" for U.S. soldiers leaving to fight in World War I, and proclaimed *The American Idea* in a show by that name. He

James Cagney, as small and lively as Cohan, began his career as a dancer and played George M. Cohan in the award-winning film version of *Yankee Doodle Dandy*.

answered his critics—who claimed he could only work with four notes—by boasting that he could write better music than other dancers and dance better than other song writers. The credo of the talented self-promoting Cohan was: "Tempo! Tempo! As much tempo as possible! That is the whole trick. Always stay in motion!" His productions and texts are distinguished by a direct style that appealed to the public and was perceived, in contrast to operetta, as modern and American. With his dynamism and theatrical instincts honed from childhood, George M. Cohan stands as the figurehead of show business.

The Revue

Although their vehement patriotism made his revues and musical comedies of less interest outside the United States, and their musical and dramatic limitations helped them fade into relative obscurity, Cohan was a true pioneer of the musical. In the 1920s, his career as producer and composer slowly wound down. He made a comeback as a performer in 1933 in the premiere of Eugene O'Neill's drama *Ah, Wilderness!* and as president Franklin D. Roosevelt in the Richard Rodgers and Lorenz Hart musical *I'd Rather Be Right* (1937). When he died in 1942, his character and music were celebrated in the film *Yankee Doodle Dandy*, for which the leading actor, James Cagney, won an Oscar. Cohan's life was also made into the 1968 musical *George M!*

In Jule Styne's 1964 *Funny Girl*, Barbra Streisand (second from right) played the legendary star of the *Ziegfeld Follies*, Fanny Brice.

The revue

Revues came into fashion near the end of the 19th century. Unlike the musical, the revue has no real story; unlike the vaudeville show, it has a specific theme. In *The Passing Show of 1894*,

the inquiries of a Manhattan detective were the pretext for sketches and musical numbers of all kinds, including a parody of the opera *Carmen*. In 1898, in Thomas Rice's *Summer Nights* a black entertainer

Stephen Sondheim's musical *Follies* (1971) used memories of the great Broadway revues as a springboard for a meditation on the transitory nature of fame and dreams.

The *Ziegfeld Follies* of *1919* (the year women were given the right to vote)–"The Declaration of the American Girl."

appeared on Broadway for the first time. Ever since the success of Lydia Thompson's British Blondes, long-legged dancers had been standard components of the most popular show numbers. Florenz Ziegfeld kept up this tradition when he presented his first *Follies* as light summer entertainment in 1907 in a Broadway rooftop garden. Indeed, it is barely possible to think of the classic extravagant Broadway revues without thinking of the name Flo Ziegfeld, or the Ziegfeld Follies. One of the Follies' biggest stars was comedienne Fanny Brice, whose big break in Ziegfeld's shows became the basis of Jule Styne's 1964 musical *Funny Girl*, which launched another extraordinarily talented Jewish New York actress—Barbra Streisand—to stardom. The revue enjoyed its heyday between 1910 and 1920, as operetta began to decline in popularity.

Jelly Roll Morton, one of the pioneers of New Orleans jazz, became the title figure of the 1992 musical *Jelly's Last Jam* with Morton's music. In the face of death, the self-styled "inventor of jazz" was confronted with having denied his African roots. Morton sees his wild life pass in review and prepares himself to die and tries to save his soul.

The era of the grand musical revue ended in the 1940s in the face of the international economic crisis and competition from radio, motion pictures, and television.

Jazz—American music

Like vaudeville and burlesque, jazz emerged from the haunts of cheap amusement and prostitution. In Storyville, the red-light district of New Orleans, each establishment had its own house musicians. The origins of jazz go back to songs that had been brought by slaves from West Africa to America since the beginning of the 17th century. African Americans joined their musical tradition with European harmony. The abolition of slavery in 1863 cleared the way for black music to reach the stage. Playing instruments like the trumpet, trombone, saxophone, or clarinet, the self-trained jazz musicians developed amazing and unorthodox techniques. Out of work music, spirituals, and marches evolved a tradition of improvisational music. Just as the Blues reflects mostly melancholy feelings, the *joi de vivre* of the early jazz musicians came across in their exuberant quickened tempo. By 1900, African-American pianists like Scott Joplin had brought their syncopated rhythms to the European piano and developed a style of their own that would soon be adopted by white composers: ragtime.

From Tin Pan Alley to Broadway:
Irving Berlin

The heart of the American musical industry, Tin Pan Alley, owes its name to a journalist, who in 1903 investigated the American music publishing houses on 28th Street in Manhattan. From the clangor of pianos emanating from open windows, his article bore the headline "Tin Pan Alley—Street of the Tin Cans." Here,

Piano edition of an early song by Irving Berlin, who as a self-taught musician could truly claim to have done it "All By Myself."

Old World, New World

Irving Berlin (1888–1989), like Cole Porter, wrote his own lyrics. George Gershwin called him "America's Franz Schubert." Berlin was one of the few composers who worked successfully in all three centers of the American music industry: Tin Pan Alley, Hollywood, and Broadway. He wrote many songs for the legendary *Ziegfeld Follies*, including the shows' anthem, "A Pretty Girl Is Like a Melody." In the 1930s he worked exclusively in Hollywood, where he produced popular songs like "Cheek to Cheek" and "White Christmas." Berlin never wrote a musical per se until 1946, when *Annie Get Your Gun* became one of the greatest successes of the day, with songs like "There's No Business Like Show Business" and "You Can't Get a Man with a Gun." This photo shows Berlin as a performer in his 1942 patriotic revue, *This Is the Army*.

salaried musicians continually composed and arranged new songs on behalf of the music publishing houses, which were distributed by so-called song pluggers through the New York bars, music halls, and theaters and offered for sale to producers, managers, singers, and bandleaders. Song pluggers were essentially the human predecessors of the demo record, tape, or CD; they traveled from venue to venue often with a portable piano and a sheaf of new sheet music which they demonstrated in an effort to sell the songs. Among the hired composers working for Tin Pan Alley were Irving Berlin, George Gershwin, and Vincent Youmans.

Irving Berlin, born Israel Baline in 1888 in Siberia as the son of a Jewish cantor, emigrated to the United States with his parents to escape the anti-Semitic pogroms; Berlin grew up poor on the Lower East Side of New York. After the early death of his father, he earned his living from the age of fourteen as a balladeer in the infamous Bowery bars and as a singing waiter in Chinatown. For the song text to "Marie from Sunny Italy," he received a whopping 37 cents in royalties, but as compensation his name appeared on the cover of the sheet music: "I. Berlin." When he offered a music publisher a song he had composed about an unhappy

Italian marathon runner named Dorando, he had to sing the melody because he could neither read nor write music. The music publisher was nevertheless impressed, hired Berlin as a songwriter, and soon made him his business partner. In 1911, Berlin had his first big hit with "Alexander's Ragtime Band," which helped introduce ragtime to the white population and triggered a popular dance craze. In the case of jazz and later rock'n' roll, black music often gained entry to main-stream American culture through a white entertainer.

Jazz on Broadway

Through jazz, American popular music and musical theater acquired their distinctive style. With jazz incorporated into stage music, the essential black element of improvisation had to be discarded. "Alexander's Ragtime Band" also domesticated ragtime: Berlin considered the authentic musical style too unorthodox for a predominantly white public. In the following years, however, jazz caught on throughout the country, and in 1914 Berlin composed the revue *Watch Your Step* exclusively in ragtime. Jazz made it possible to fuse European and American elements into the musical. From 1910 to 1920, revues had gained consider-able popularity, and around the time of World War I, the musicals of Jerome Kern, George Gershwin, and Vincent Youmans rivaled oper-ettas in popularity. Within a few years, Broad-way suddenly boasted a whole generation of young, American-born (or reared) composers, inspired by jazz and an American outlook on life.

Irving Berlin may well be considered the greatest American inventor of melody in the entertainment industry. His lyrics amaze with their original simplicity. He saw him-self modestly as a songwriter, nothing more, nothing less. Of the more than a thou-sand songs he published in a career that spanned six decades, he insisted, "most of these songs were bad, or at least amateurish." The title of one of his earliest songs might well have served as a lifelong motto for the composer, "Play A Simple Melody."

"The American theater is five street blocks long and one and a half blocks wide," proclaimed American playwright Arthur Miller. In fact, "Broadway" extends north to 59th Street, south to 40th Street, east to Avenue of the Americas (6th Avenue), and west to 9th Avenue—midway, between 7th and 8th Avenues, runs Broadway itself, the Great White Way. Broadway has been the center of the American theater ever since New York supplanted Philadelphia around 1830 as the preeminent home of the stage. Although other American cities may boast internationally renowned opera houses, dance companies, and theater companies, the success of a show has for a long time been measured exclusively by the length of its run and the amount of its profits on Broadway. The universality of this truth is expressed in the song "New York, New York"—"If I can make it there, I'll make it anywhere."

The rules and mechanisms under which the Broadway theater emerged have remained essentially unchanged since the 19th century. The central figure in the market-economy-oriented American theater is the producer. Unable to rely on state subsidies, the producer finances projects by enlisting investors. Each production is set up like a stock holding corporation. The financiers, known in Broadway jargon as "angels," purchase shares (points) of the production, which may yield considerable profits. For example, in 1943 the investors in *Oklahoma!* received a return of $35 for every dollar invested. The angels may also, more often than not, kiss their money goodbye.

The "angels" used to be in most cases private individuals who bet on shows as they would bet on a horse,

On Broadway: The Majestic Theater in the 1980s.

Winter Garden and Broadway. New York City.

Broadway, 1916. The original Winter Garden, the home of the great revues.

and were cultivated by producers into patrons of the arts. Nowadays most investors use business managers and corporations, primarily film companies, who hope, if not for profits, then for useful tax write-offs.

Out of ten productions, only one or two show a profit after expenses. To keep the risk of losses to a minimum, Broadway premieres take place only after extended tryouts around the country—traditionally in cities like Boston or Baltimore or Detroit—and after a short period of previews in New York. The pre-opening performances are more for the benefit of the director and cast, who may make changes in response to audience reactions. A show succeeds or fails, however, based on the reviews and box office sales of its Broadway premiere. Only rarely does a musical prevail against the vote of the mighty New York drama critics. While artistic decisions are supposedly left to the director and producer(s), large investors may wield some clout as well. Composers and authors as a rule will accede to these demands. So, in 1924, George Gershwin reluctantly cut the song "The Man I Love" from *Lady,*

Be Good! because a potential investor threatened to withdraw his money if the song remained in the show. The sacrifice was for nothing: The investor bailed out anyway. "The Man I Love," on the other hand, became one of Gershwin's best-known songs. Even the multimillionaire Cole Porter, only two years after his box-office success with *Kiss Me, Kate,* submitted to the rules of the trade, and against his artistic judgment replaced several of his favorite songs from *Out of This World* with new compositions. Broadway works according to the principle of hire and fire: Nothing and no one is irreplaceable. If the producer does not fix up the show, a play doctor is hired who sometimes rewrites the entire script. Stars, no less than ensemble members, can be replaced at the drop of a hat; very few are so valuable to a production that they can set their own conditions (though, of course, some are, or manage to be sure they are treated as such). Between the actual opening in Baltimore or Toronto and the all-important New York premiere, weeks or months can pass; some productions may meet such devastating audience reactions on the way that they never reach Broadway; it may be cheaper to put the production down than to fix it. The premiere of Andrew Lloyd Webber's new musical *Whistle Down the Wind* was first announced for April, then for June 1997, and was finally delayed indefinitely after bad reviews. The show, if it ever reaches New York, will likely be fundamentally revised.

The King and I, by Richard Rodgers and Oscar Hammerstein, opened in 1951 and was successfully revived on Broadway in 1996–97.

To mount the production, auditions are held for singers, dancers, and actors. The stage and film musical *A Chorus Line* (1975) depicts an open audition—called a "cattle call"—for the dance ensemble of a production. Soloists are selected in separate auditions. Of course, it is easier to recruit investors, often through staged 'readings' by cast members, if the producer can boast a star performer to augment known composers and authors.

Theaters in the United States are generally privately owned, though not, as a rule, by producers. Rather, producers currently rent the theater for an average $8,500 per day. The Shubert brothers were among the most famous theater owners who were also active producers: In 1949 they owned 15 of 32 Broadway stages, as well as over 100 theaters in other cities. This system spares producers the expense of maintaining a large ensemble or production staff. However, union rules (and the unions are quite strong in the theater and entertainment businesses) often require that each production employ more technicians and musicians than are really needed. In addition, technicians' jobs are closely defined and circumscribed, and union rules forbid members to perform duties that are not spelled out in their contracts. The unions may also interfere in casting questions: A storm of controversy ensued when British actor Jonathan Pryce was engaged for the Broadway production of *Miss Saigon*: There was strong pressure from the public and Actors' Equity to cast an Asian-American actor in the role of a Vietnamese, since this ethnic minority otherwise has little opportunity for major roles. The issue stymied production until a fairly complicated compromise was reached.

High theater rents and the power of the unions have in the course of recent decades led to skyrocketing costs. Where the 1949 production of Jule Styne's *Gentlemen Prefer Blondes* cost $160,000, the Walt Disney production of *Beauty and the Beast* in the mid-1990s, devoured $16 million. In fairness, however, Broadway theater has also experienced a phenomenon that can only be described as "Can You Top This?," with spectacle—scenery, costumes, effects—eating an ever-increasing chunk of the production budget.

Only commercial success counts on Broadway: Musicals cater to the market, not necessarily to posterity or any loftier artistic ideals. Like the trend of remaking old Hollywood films, so, too, Broadway has found it increasingly profitable to revive old shows whose book and music have stood the test of time. Examples include revivals in recent years of Frank Loesser's *Guys and Dolls*, Stephen Sondheim's *A Funny Thing Happened on the Way to the Forum*, and the newest reentry in the 1996-97 season, Jerome Kern and Oscar Hammerstein's 70-year-old *Showboat*—all of which have been celebrated triumphs. However, a musical that fails at its premiere is rarely revived. The exception that proves the rule, Leonard Bernstein's ambitious 1957 musical *Candide*, based on the novel of the French Enlightenment philosopher Voltaire, closed after only 73 performances. Its

1974 revival ran over 10 times as long. Broadway does not have repertory theater with productions that change daily—the costs of changing the sets and maintaining a standing ensemble are prohibitive. Commercial theater is seen as a theater for the general public—albeit a public willing to pay a top ticket price of $65 or more for an orchestra seat. That means a demanding schedule: eight shows a week, six evenings (Tuesday to Sunday) as well as two afternoon matinees. The cast of a successful production may well have to perform on stage every day except Monday for years—although few leads will stay with even a successful production for that long. Understudies who have studied and rehearsed specific roles must stay prepared to step in if a principal should be ill; second- or third-string players,

Poster for the 1980 Broadway production of *42nd Street*.

on the other hand, may have to remain ready to play any supporting or ensemble part that comes up at a moment's notice—the chorus and dance ensembles include so-called swings, who can take over several parts if necessary.

Broadway is a vital commercial district, home not only to theaters and production companies, but to count-less private artists' agencies, dance studios, drama schools, stagecraft workshops, or audio engineering companies who have settled there where the action is. Few theatrical genres are as intimately associated with a specific place as the musical is with Broadway, though it has also been the site of premieres by the most important American drama-tists—from Eugene O'Neill to Ten-nessee Williams to Tony Kushner.

An audition with producer George Abbott for Mary Rodgers's *Once Upon a Mattress* (1959).

Their works are produced under the same commercial conditions as musi-cals. With the ever-growing ticket prices, however, the literary theater leads more and more of a shadowy existence, with serious works often only attracting a good house by featuring movie and television stars. Indeed, the so-called legitimate theater in America may well be con-sidered decentralized, with Broad-way not really its home anymore.

What the Oscar is to Hollywood, the Antoinette Perry Award, or "Tony," is to Broadway. Each year, since the 1946/47 season, these coveted prizes have been awarded to the Best Musical and Best Drama (indeed, a new category—Best Re-vival—was added in recent years), as well as to composers, authors, direc-tors, performers, producers, de-signers, and choreographers. And just as Alfred Hitchcock never won an Oscar for best director, Leonard Bernstein's masterpiece *West Side*

The Broadway Theater.

Story came away empty-handed in 1957/58 (though the film version was appropriately honored by the Academy Awards): In that season, Meredith Willson's *The Music Man* won the Tony for best musical.

Since the early 1950s, Off-Broadway theaters have in principle functioned according to the same private-sector rules as Broadway. Off-Broadway means, first of all, a location somewhere outside that central slice of Manhattan delineated earlier, and primarily theaters with fewer than 300 seats whose commercial success is measured accordingly. These venues are more often home to experimental drama, or sometimes give new writers and composers a chance to cut their teeth. The road to mainstream Broadway, after all, is never clear-cut. *The Fantasticks*, a minimal, sweet, innocent musical by Harvey Schmidt and Tom Jones, ran since its premiere in 1960 for about 15,000 performances at the small Sullivan Street Playhouse in Greenwich Village. The sexually daring success *Oh, Calcutta* (cowritten by theater critic Kenneth Tynan) managed to make the leap to Broadway from Off-Broadway in 1969, as did *Hair*, which started its life at Joseph Papp's New York Shakespeare Festival Public Theatre; and the 1996 Tony Award winner, *Rent*, was first produced in a 99-seat theater.

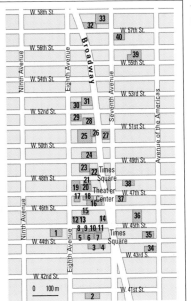

The theaters and concert halls around Broadway and Times Square

1 The Martin Beck
2 The Nederlander
3 The St. James
4 The Helen Hayes
5 The Majestic
6 The Broadhurst
7 The Shubert
8 The John Golden
9 The Royale
10 The Plymouth
11 The Booth
12 The Imperial
13 The Music Box
14 The Minskoff
15 The 46th Street
16 The Lunt-Fontanne
17 The Brooks Atkinson
18 The Edison
19 The Biltmore
20 The Ethel Barrymore
21 The Longacre
22 The Ritz
23 The Eugene O'Neill
24 The Ambassador
25 The Circle in the Square
26 The George Gershwin
27 The Winter Garden
28 The Mark Hellinger
29 The Neil Simon
30 The Virginia
31 The Broadway
32 The Lincoln Art
33 The American Fine Arts
34 Town Hall
35 The Belasco
36 The Lyceum
37 The Palace
38 The Cort
39 New York City Center
40 Carnegie Hall

1918 – 1929

The Jazz Age

America after the First World War

On April 6, 1917, after attacks by German U-boats killed American citizens, the United States entered the First World War. The end of the war was also the end of European prim-acy: The United States emerged as the leading world power. Economic-ally, it was al-ready the leader: Between 1860 and 1914 the population had

grown from 31.3 to 91.9 million and economic production had increased about twentyfold.

The 1920s began as a decade of almost boundless optimism—known in the history of civilization as the "Jazz Age"—and it ended with the stock market crash of 1929. The previously dominant influence of Europe was displaced by a self-confident American culture; with the introduction of "talkies," Hollywood became the undisputed center of the motion picture industry, a position it would hold indefinitely. In other arts, an American voice, or vision, began to emerge: Edward Hopper painted the landscape of the New World—including its diners and gas stations, with strokes of soft realism; architect Frank Lloyd Wright carved a sober modern style. Eugene O'Neill stepped into the vacuum of the American theater by becoming the nation's first world-class dramatist; and in novel-ist F. Scott Fitzgerald the Jazz Age found a chronicler.

Meanwhile, jazz—that uniquely American musical form—was conquering not only the New

World's large cities—Chicago, New York—but also the music and dance halls of the Old World, where it shook up the standing model of European musical theater.

Eubie Blake's *Shuffle Along* was in 1921 the first musical composed and performed by African Americans to open on Broadway. At its premiere, Paul Robeson—an operatic bass who became an icon of "serious" black performers—was a member of a singing quartet and the legendary Josephine Baker danced in the chorus. Now, for the first time, blacks were allowed to sit together with whites on the theater floor—there was a time when they were restricted to the balconies. Another first was a love duet between black partners—not a parody in a minstrel show, but as a sincere dramatic moment. The rousing jazz and the breathtaking choreography of *Shuffle Along* impressed the young white composers, who prepared to re-new the American musical theater with their musical comedies. The "classics" of the musical—Irving Berlin, George Gershwin, Jerome Kern,

Left:
A scene from Eubie Blake's
Shuffle Along (1921).

1918 - 1929

Cole Porter, and Richard Rodgers—had all written Broadway musicals prior to 1920. While Ber-lin was still writing ex-clusively for revues, and Porter preferred to lead a luxurious life in Europe writing musical scores, Gershwin, Kern, and Rodgers were already making a mark on American musical theater in the 1920s.

"Flappers." Sandy Wilson's 1954 musical *The Boy Friend* lovingly and nostalgically parodied the light musical comedies of the 1920s.

1918 – 1929

With anarchic comedies like *Animal Crackers*, the Marx Brothers were among the most popular stage entertainers of the 1920s. Irving Berlin wrote the music for *The Cocoanuts* in 1925. In the 1920s, Groucho, Chico, and Harpo (and their straight-men brothers Zeppo and Gummo on occasion) worked in Hollywood, where they made movie versions of their stage successes, and then "original" movies, which usually included some song and dance and always Harpo playing the harp and Chico playing the piano. The 1970 musical *Minnie's Boys* revolved around their early years and their mother Minnie's role in their careers.

Musical comedies

Most of these composers learned their craft working as "song pluggers" for music publishing houses and as rehearsal pianists in theaters. Their swinging and optimistic melodies reflected the tempo and spirit of the Jazz Age. The new generation opposed the backward-looking, rosy view of the operetta—with its beloved student choruses, wild desert sons, and delicate princesses; they preferred a picture of contemporary America. The result is that even today the music seems fresh, original, and inspired, while, as a rule, the books (the general term for the story—text, dialogue, plot, etc.—of a musical play) seem shallow and insubstantial—evidence that the book was originally nothing more than a pretext (like the supposed themes of musical revues) for the music and dancing, much as the plots of Marx Brothers movies were a superficial excuse for comedic shenanigans. The flimsy stories were of amorous complications in the world of the rich and beautiful or of ever-happily surmounted difficulties. Many songs were written before the action and plot had been completely decided. Often the songs were not completely integrated into the dramatic context, and the lyrics sometimes flagrantly contradicted the spoken dialogue. So it could happen that a young woman could sing of a great love that—hopefully!—would soon arrive, although she had already fallen in love in the previous scene with the man the authors intended for her. Oscar Hammerstein, who in 1925 wrote the book for Jerome Kern's musical *Sunny*, recalled how the producer chose the performers as if assembling acts for a revue: In one typical instance, a ukulele virtuoso was signed, but his contract stipulated that he would appear between 10:00 and 10:10 p.m.; "art," clearly, had nothing to do with it. The authors therefore had to write the show to accommodate this contractual term so that Ukelele Ike would appear on stage at just the right time. The thinness of the stories, characters, and plots explains why many of the musical comedies of the 1920s are never revived, indeed, most are unknown, though the music may well have survived—recycled into newer productions with new stories or rediscovered in the boom of recorded music of the second half of the century. Occasionally an old show may be appreciated for its intentional absurdity, but most are best forgotten as the lint that they were.

Jazz, with its dynamic off-beat (emphasis on the 2nd and 4th beats instead of the 1st and 3rd as in European music) laid the foundation of the musical songs of the 1920s.

George Gershwin

Like Irving Berlin, George Gershwin's family emigrated from Russia, though Gershwin himself was born in Brooklyn in 1898. His middle-class parents originally intended their older son Ira to take piano lessons, but Ira, two years older than George, showed little interest in the instrument. By the age of fifteen, George was working as a song plugger, and the music publisher Max Dreyfus, who, with his brother Louis, was one of the most influential men of the industry, soon hired Gershwin as a paid composer. Gershwin spent his breaks, to the surprise of his colleagues, studying J.S. Bach's *Well-Tempered Klavier*. Lacking academic education, Gershwin knew no hierarchy of the different musical forms. He hungrily assimilated everything that came to his ears:

George Gershwin (1898–1937).

jazz, classical, popular hits, and theater music. Occasionally he managed to place one or another of his early songs in a Broadway show. In 1918, Al Jolson, then starring in musical revues, added Gershwin's song *Swanee* to his repertoire and helped the composer to his first nationwide hit. Gershwin contributed many compositions to the annual revue *George White's Scandals* between 1920 and 1924. One of his most extraordinary contributions in 1922 was a 20-minute "Opera à la Afro-American" called *Blue Monday Blues*, which was interpreted in minstrel tradition by white actors in blackface. The ambitious and un-usually long work caused some irritation and

was cancelled after the premiere; still, *Blue Monday Blues* gave a foretaste of Gershwin's jazz opera *Porgy and Bess*, which he would write thirteen years later.

With the 1924 *Rhapsody in Blue*, Gershwin achieved a successful fusion of jazz and classical styles: "In the *Rhapsody*, I tried to express our manner of living, the tempo of our modern life with its speed and chaos and vitality. ... Composers assimilate influences and suggestions from various sources and even borrow from one another's works. That's

Al Jolson in the "oriental" review *Sinbad*, which popularized Gershwin's song "Swanee."

why I consider the *Rhapsody* as embodying an assimilation of feeling." Now, for the first time, a hit composer from Tin Pan Alley also appeared in international concert halls and achieved recognition in the "serious" music world. In the same year, Gershwin celebrated his first musical success on Broadway with *Lady, Be Good!* The

show belongs among the better musical comedies of the 1920s not only because of Gershwin's music, but also because of the witty, absurd dialogue of British librettist Guy Bolton. Gershwin's brother Ira wrote the song lyrics, whose careless, self-ironical colloquialism set them far above the level of most texts of the time and correspond to the jazz idiom of the music. George and Ira as collaborators enjoyed a close relationship that allowed them to work together in a way and with an intensity not typical of most song writing teams. Ira Gershwin established himself as one of the most original lyricists of his time. The action of *Lady, Be Good!*, however, is typical of the flippant, devil-may-care musical comedies of the 1920s: A dancing and singing brother and sister pair are evicted from their apartment five years before the stock market crash of 1929 that plunged the world into an international economic crisis. Still, neither homelessness nor prohibition can spoil the good mood. Luckily, there are parties for dancing the wild Charleston, bootleggers to inject a little intrigue, and some not too entangled love and financial affairs, resulting in an amorous and lucrative happy ending. The stars of *Lady, Be Good!* were the real-life brother-and-sister pair, Fred and Adele Astaire. Gershwin took into account Astaire's limited vocal abilities when he wrote

George Gershwin's 1924 *Lady, Be Good!* with Fred Astaire and his sister Adele.

A Mexican bootlegger and a self-confident socialite: Gershwin's *Lady, Be Good!* in a 1997 revival in Berlin.

the singing part for the dancer. The result was a casual spoken singing style that, unlike the more classical operetta style, suited the light, modern jazzy style and is still a good model for musical comedy singers. The prevalent AABA song form enabled the authors to emphasize points in the story or to give romantic histories in songs: After an introduction of at most eight bars comes the main theme, which is repeated, followed by another eight-bar section called the bridge, and then repeated again. This formula underlies most songs of the classic musicals.

Two of the greatest musical stars began their careers in Gershwin's *Girl Crazy* (1930): Ginger Rogers (right) debuted as the love-struck messenger girl and pursued her career in Hollywood ...

In the ensuing years, Gershwin composed the music for a series of these lighthearted musical comedies. His songs for *Girl Crazy* were arranged for a jazz ensemble, and at the premiere on October 14, 1930, the elite of the the country's white jazz musicians sat in the orchestra pit: the Red Nichols Orchestra with Benny Goodman, Gene Krupa, Glenn Miller, Jimmy Dorsey, and Jack Teagarden.

The jazz influence is readily heard in Gershwin's strongly syncopated, swinging music, as it is in other composers of his generation. George and Ira Gershwin's first joint song in 1918 had the programmatic title "The Real American Folksong Is a Rag." The popularity of their theater music went far beyond the shows for which it was written; many Gershwin compositions were played and recorded and improvised upon by jazz musicians. Even if we set aside nostalgia, Gershwin's songs today retain their original vitality and lightness. Although he was well-versed in a wide range of musical styles, his own style is unmistakable, whether in an orchestral work or in a song for a musical

... and Ethel Merman stopped the show with her spirited rendition of the show's best and most popular song, "I Got Rhythm."

comedy. Two successful revivals, *My One and Only* (1983) and *Crazy For You* (1992), prove that George Gershwin's elegant music still sounds fresh and lively.

In 1927, in *Strike Up the Band*, George and Ira Gershwin teamed up with the renowned librettist George S. Kaufman and tried to counter the superficiality of their previous shows with a sharper, more satirical tone. The public, however, was not quite ready for this: the show closed out of town and did not reach Broadway until 1930, just as the Depression was grabbing hold of the country, and then it arrived in a somewhat revised form.

Alongside his work on musical comedies, Gershwin continued to compose classical orchestral works like *An American in Paris* and the *Concerto in F for Piano*. Toward the end of the 1920s, he mentioned to the Russian emigré Igor Stravinsky that he would like to study with him. Stravinsky (with a reputation for over-fussiness about matters of dollars and cents) asked Gershwin how much he earned and Gershwin

Under the title *Crazy For You*, a new version of *Girl Crazy* came to Broadway in 1992 and also won an enthusiastic audience as a touring production. The largely revised plot winkingly refers to the clichés of musical comedy: Young man from good family wants to be in the theater, mother banishes him to Nevada where he puts on a show in an old vaudeville house with imported dancing girls and genuine cowboys, and after some misunderstandings wins the heart of the theater owner's daughter.

Vincent Youmans (1898–1946) came from a well-to-do New York family and initially had little ambition for a career in music or theater. One of his melodies, however, happened into the hands of John Philip Sousa, the composer of patriotic marches and director of the U.S. Navy band. When Youmans heard his pieces played by a big band, he abandoned his previous plans to be an engineer.

gave an approximate answer, which must have quite impressed the Russian, who replied dryly, "In that case, I should study with you." Gershwin's two composing careers converged in 1935, two years before his death at the age of 39, with his jazz opera *Porgy and Bess*.

Vincent Youmans

One year after Gershwin's *Lady, Be Good!*, the younger (by one day) Vincent Youmans came out with his first great Broadway success, *No, No, Nanette*. No doubt this musical comedy's most famous song, "Tea for Two" was added first at the urging of the producer during tryouts. Much to the horror of lyricist Irving Caesar, the song was hustled into the show with the "dummy text"—composers often wrote the tunes before the script was finished; the lyricist would supply words that corresponded to the song's rhythm and accents, with little meaning or connection to the song's ultimate context. "Tea for Two" retained its dummy text with almost no changes. The melody is musically ingenious and clear: The whole song is based on the rhythmic pattern—dotted quarter, eighth note, that is, long-short, long-short.

No, No, Nanette was performed and celebrated out of town before its official Broadway premiere for over a year—to the point where the New York press grumbled: "Boston's seen it, Philadelphia's seen it, Chicago's seen it, London's seen it, and presumably also Guatemala, Medicine Bend and the Canary Islands have already seen it." After a long run on Broadway, No, No, Nanette toured the United States, and then to enthusiastic houses in Europe, South America, and Asia. It became the most-performed musical of the 1920s and a 1971 revival was also a huge hit. Youmans's only other major success was the 1927 sailor comedy *Hit the Deck*.

Another popular song from *No, No, Nanette* was "I Want To Be Happy." But despite his early successes, Youmans's early promise was never really fulfilled. Like F. Scott Fitzgerald, he became a member of the "lost generation." Suffering from tuberculosis since childhood, he seemed to be unable to handle his immense talent. He succumbed to alcoholism and deteriorated from the good-looking and charming party goer to a moody loner. He was never successful in developing a collaboration with a competent lyricist. His ambitious and costly *Rainbow*, based on the 1849 California gold rush, opened in November 1928. It was a disaster in no uncertain terms: The first act lasted nearly three hours, a mule balked onstage, slowing down the already ponderous production, and Youmans had to cancel the only love duet after a furious quarrel with the producer shortly before the opening night. All in all, the public was not inclined to embrace such a demanding show for its time, and *Rainbow* closed after only 30 performances. From then on, Youmans decided to act as his own producer; true to form, unfortunately, he quarrelled with with almost all his writers, producers, performers, and costume designers. His ensuing productions also flopped. On top of these personal failures, his family lost their wealth in the stock market crash. His tuberculosis forced Youmans into more frequent sanitarium stays and

Youmans's *Hit the Deck* is a sailor comedy. It tells the story of the coffee house proprietress Loulou who falls in love with the sailor Bilge. He refuses to marry Loulou when he learns she is an heiress but relents when she signs her fortune over to her children.

Richard Rodgers (left) and Lorenz Hart (right). For the disciplined composer Rodgers, the genial Bohemian Hart was a "Partner, friend and constant source of irritation."

1918 – 1929

longer breaks from work. *Hit the Deck* remained his last success on Broadway. He died April 5, 1946 at the age of 47 in a hotel in Denver.

The operetta tradition

Although the operetta was essentially passé by the late 1920s, early 1930s, works by composers like Romberg, Herbert and Friml still managed to find some success. These were works that managed to remain relatively untouched by the jazzy orientation of George Gershwin, Cole Porter, or Harold Arlen, musicals influenced instead by the operetta tradition. In fact, one could think of the more operetta-influenced musicals as following a parallel track to the jazz works. Many of the names are now forgotten, but many are not, and probably the most important composer along these lines is Richard Rodgers. At the peak of this tradition is Lerner and Loewe's *My Fair Lady*.

Richard Rodgers was born in 1902, the son of a Long Island doctor. In 1915, when he saw Jerome Kern's *Very Good Eddie*, he decided he wanted to compose theater music. For a holiday review in the following year, the 14-year old wrote his first song. In 1918, he and some friends wanted to bring an amateur production to the stage, and he went in search of a lyricist. Among his acquaintances was his future partner Oscar Hammerstein, who had to withdraw from this early theatrical venture because his uncle, an influential Broadway producer, had found him a job as a temporary pianist. Hammerstein was replaced by Lorenz Hart, who became Rodger's ideal partner and friend. Hart was born in 1895 in New York (a great-nephew of the German poet Heinrich Heine); his first theatrical experience was translating German operetta libretti. The song "Any Old Place with You" from one of their amateur reviews was bought by the prominent producer Lew Fields in 1919 for a Broadway show. Although Fields's next production, *Poor Little Rich Girl*, had dramatic songs composed by Sigmund Romberg, Fields hired Rodgers and Hart for seven lighter songs. In 1927, encouraged by the success of their music for a revue called the *Garrick Gaieties*, which, like an amateur show, gave young talent a chance to be heard, Rodgers and Hart took on their most demanding project to date: a musical comedy, based on Mark Twain's *A Connecticut Yankee in King Arthur's Court*.

1918 – 1929

The milestone: *Show Boat*

By 1927, the time was evidently ripe for more serious themes on Broadway. While Gershwin worked as a concert composer and began

thinking about a jazz opera, and Rodgers and Hart made their mark with *A Connecticut Yankee*, Jerome Kern set a milestone in the development of the musical with *Show Boat*.

Show Boat (scene photo from a Broadway-Revival) by Jerome Kern and Oscar Hammerstein is considered by many the first genuine American musical.

Immediately after its premiere on December 27, 1927, the show was greeted as a masterpiece by the critics, the public, and the theater world. Kern and his collaborator Oscar Hammerstein (who wrote the book and lyrics) based *Show Boat* on a novel by Edna Ferber. The action spanned over four decades, with many scene changes, and treated atypical subjects for musical theater like racial discrimination and alienation between marriage partners. At the

1918 – 1929

same time, the material offered a self-reflection on show business. *Show Boat* is the first book musical in which the musical numbers spring directly from the plot: Songs occur when the emotions are so great or the situation so poignant or the voices so intense that words no longer suffice.

Music as the vessel of the plot

Jerome Kern (1885–1945) studied music at the beginning of the 20th century in New York and Germany. Between 1905 and 1912, he adapted European operetta imports for the American public; during this time he was occasionally asked to augment the scores with his own works. In 1915 he was given a chance to develop his own musicals for the small, 300-seat Princess Theater. Kern had come to believe, even at this early point in his career, that the musical numbers should forward the action of the piece and should suit the characters of the dramatic figures. Kern, with librettist Guy Bolton, pursued this conviction in the musical comedies he developed for the Princess Theater. Their first work, *Very Good Eddie*, which was produced in 1915, inspired both the 13-year-old Richard Rodgers and the 17-year-old George Gershwin. With British humorist and songwriter P. G. Wodehouse, the Kern-Bolton duo became a trio. Their light comedies *Oh, Boy!*, *Leave It to Jane*, and *Oh, Lady! Lady!!* were groundbreaking in their integration of the dramatic action with the songs and dance numbers. The humor emerged from the situations and characters, rather than relying on actors' slapstick or clowning, as was more standard fare at the time. For a while, however, Kern's work and his dramaturgical ideas met with a cool reception from a public hungry for hits, whether integrated into the drama or utter non sequiturs.

Original poster design for *Very Good Eddie* (1915), which may be considered one of the first musical comedies, with a plot that served as a transparent pretext for the presentation of musical and dance numbers. The academically trained composer Jerome Kern combined the European operetta tradition, in which he was rooted, with authentic American folklore. Kern was a model and father figure for the young generation of composers of the 1920s.

Kern's music for two variations on the Cinderella story, the musical comedies *Sally* (1920) and *Sunny* (1925), contributed to their popular success, but as theater works, the two pieces—with

From around 1915 through the early to mid-1920s, Guy Bolton, P. G. Wodehouse, and Jerome Kern (from the left) created a series of impeccable musical comedies.

somewhat cliché-riddled books—represented throwbacks for the Princess Theater. Kern did not give up, however, and he eventually brought in the undisputed revue king and professed experimentalist, Florenz Ziegfeld, to produce *Show Boat*.

The first book musical

The "Show Boat" of the title is one of the luxurious wooden paddle-wheel pleasure palaces that traveled up and down the Mississippi River in the late 19th century. Some were gambling halls, and others, like Captain Andy's *Cotton Blossom* in *Show Boat*, were vaudeville theaters. If "Life Upon the Wicked Stage" (to quote one of the show's songs) was difficult, the life of the black longshoremen on the river was much harder. Magnolia, Captain Andy's daughter, and the roving gambler Ravenal fall in love at first sight. When the star of the *Cotton Blossom*, the mixed-race Julie, is driven away after her forbidden marriage to the white Steve is revealed (miscegenation was a crime in Mississippi at the time), Magnolia and Ravenal replace Julie and Steve on stage. The initially happy marriage between Magnolia and Ravenal is corroded by his gambling fever; he leaves her and their daughter Kim. Years later, Magnolia appears in a night club in Chicago, where she

Show Boat took as its subject racial and marital conflict, but it also offered theater on theater, and one of the first reflections on show business. Oscar Hammerstein's book used the clash of reality and stage to dramatic effects. Scene photo from the original 1927 production.

1918 – 1929

steps in for Julie once again: Julie also has been left by Steve and, embittered by years of racist abuse, descended into alcoholism. In 1927, Magnolia's daughter Kim has become a musical star. On Captain Andy's new show boat, after decades of separation, Magnolia and Ravenal are happily reunited.

When, after the overture, the curtain opened on the first act, the first-night public looked upon the usual ensemble scene, but instead of long-legged showgirls, the chorus of black longshoremen sang out: "Niggers all work on the Mississippi, while the white folks play" (these are the original words—they were tempered mid-century to "colored folks" but restored in the recent revival). This theme is taken up again shortly in *Show Boat*'s most famous song, "Ol' Man River." The song takes up the hard life of those who work on the river, whose grief feels eternal: "I gets weary and sick of tryin', I'm tired of livin', and feared of dyin', but Ol' Man River, he jest keeps rollin' along."

The opening of the first act is a grand example for musical theater authors and composers: the songs and en-

Several movie versions were made of *Show Boat*. In the 1951 film, Marge and Gower Champion played the dance pair Ellie and Frank, who appear on the show boat. Gower Champion later became a successful Broadway director, honored posthumously with a Tony Award for a revival of *42nd Street*.

sembles establish the atmosphere, the characters and their conflicts are laid out. The music unobtrusively drives the action forward. In the first encounter between Magnolia and Ravenal, the lovers sing of their emerging love in the duet "Make Believe," whose dialogue-like structure, with changing meters and musical motifs, externalizes the internal processes of the characters. Kern uses a wide range of musical styles in *Show Boat*: Beside southern black folklore and Negro spirituals in "Ol' Man River" or "Can't

Help Loving Dat Man," Kern's duets between Magnolia and Gaylord ring with unmistakable operetta elements like waltz time and introductions reminiscent of Offenbach.

Show Boat set new, unexpected standards for musical theater in its fusion of content and atmospheric elements. For example, in the softly ironic ballad "Bill," which Kern wrote with P. G. Wodehouse in 1918 for *Oh, Lady! Lady!!*, Julie sings onstage of her dream man, for whom she had always longed, but then "along came Bill," who was nothing like her ideal. In the first act of the show, Julie sang "Can't Help Lovin' Dat Man," expressing her helplessness and inability to do anything but love a man who does not treat her well. She sings "Bill" in the second act, after she has been abandoned by her husband Steve (whom she associates with "Bill"). The amusing song text—"I can't explain/ It's surely not his brain,/That makes me thrill"—takes on a deeper, more poignant dimension.

Few musicals have been revived as often as *Show Boat*. Rehearsal photo from a 1971 revival.

Kern's compositions transcend effective theater music: He was able to write enduring hits like "Ol' Man River," whose ever-developing melodies seem to grow organically rather than coming across as a composer's artificial inventions. Occasionally he employed unusual harmonies (as in an often-cut slave chorus) and heavily syncopated rhythms. Kern said that he often worked for hours on a simple musical phrase, adding variations and inversions, until the melody had that almost symphonic quality that other composers so admired in his songs.

Despite all the show's innovations, the librettist Oscar Hammerstein still followed some musical comedy conventions and wrote—contrary to

1918 – 1929

Edna Ferber's novel—a happy ending for Magnolia and Ravenal. That *Show Boat*, nonetheless, represented a giant step toward the musical as an independent and enduring art form was unmistakable. It was also an economic success, so much so that Ziegfeld even considered renting another theater and running it simultaneously on two stages. The touring company and the London production attracted audiences as large as those on Broadway, where it was again produced in 1932. It is surprising, however, that *Show Boat*'s successful formula was only tentatively imitated—its real heirs, Gershwin's *Porgy and Bess* and some of Rodgers and Hart's carefully plotted pieces, would not come out until the end of the 1930s, nearly a decade after Kern and Hammerstein's great leap forward.

Even Kern himself did not follow in his own footsteps. After the pioneering and indelible achievements of *Show Boat*, his subsequent work relapsed into the conventions of operetta or shallow musical comedies. *Roberta* (1933), set in the Paris fashion world, warrants greater interest, thanks mainly to Kern's music, especially the ballad "Smoke Gets in Your Eyes," one of his most famous songs. After 1934, Kern worked in Hollywood on film music and adaptations of his previous pieces. At the time of his unexpected death on November 11, 1945, he had just agreed to work again with his long-time friend Oscar Hammerstein on the music for what would become *Annie Get Your*

Jerome Kern's *Roberta* was filmed in 1935 with Fred Astaire and Ginger Rogers. Kern himself worked predominantly in Hollywood during the 1930s.

1918 - 1929

Gun, which ultimately ended in the hands of Irving Berlin.

All-singing! All-dancing! All-talking!

The year 1927 brought another landmark event that would reverberate, for better or worse, through the American musical theater world. With the smashing success of *The Jazz Singer*, the sound film, or talkie, took the world of popular entertainment by storm. It also stamped the origin of the genre of the movie musical: leading actor Al Jolson not only spoke the prophetic sentence, "You ain't heard nothing yet!," he also sang several songs. Sound film technology had been available since the early 1920s but did not catch on until, in an act of desperation, the financially troubled Warner Brothers film studio staked everything on the *The Jazz Singer*, and won. The previously skeptical movie industry now saw undeniably that the revolutionary technology could no longer be held back, and by 1930 the sound movie had prevailed completely in the United States and Western Europe. Within a few years all major Broadway musicals were made into movies. Because of the lower cost of a movie ticket, Hollywood could now compete with Broadway, and wooed away composers, lyricists, authors, and performers. The next blow to the New York theater system came two years later when, on October 25, 1929, the New York Stock Exchange crashed and triggered the Great Depression.

The motion picture industry quickly realized that musicals and revues were well suited to the new talking-picture technology. In *Hollywood Review* (1929), Jacques Haley, Marion Davies, and the great silent movie comedian Buster Keaton gave the first-ever performance of *Singin' in the Rain.*

The shift from silent movies to talkies is the subject of one of the most beautiful movie musicals, *Singin' in the Rain* (1952), by Stanley Donen and Gene Kelly. The careers of silent movie stars Don Lockwood and Lina Lamont are seriously threatened by talkies, primarily because Lina, with her nasal voice and lower-class accent and vernacular speech, is hardly right for the roles of great ladies she acted in silents. The problems of the new technology and Lina's language insufficiencies turn a test shooting into a hilarious farce. However, Lockwood, with his friend Cosmo Brown and the girl he loves, Kathy Seldon, come up with a solution: What was originally written as a costume drama becomes a film musical, with the help of jazzy music and fantastic choreography and Kathy Seldon offstage singing and speaking for Lina Lamont, who only lip-synchs. (Ironically, Debbie Reynolds, who played Kathy Seldon, actually lip-synched the songs, while the vocally accomplished Jean Hagen, who played Lina Lamont, was dubbed in.)

Although successful musical plays had also been made into silent pictures, the genre of the movie musical could really only get underway with the development of sound film technology. Hollywood quickly grasped that musical comedies were ideally suited to the possibilities of the new medium. In Europe as well, musical films were being made. In France, René Clair established the genre with films like

Sous les toits de Paris (1930), while in Germany Willy Fritsch and Lilian Harvey starred in *Die drei von der Tankstelle* (1930) or *Der Kongress tanzt* (1931), with music by Werner Richard Heymann. Reinhold Schänzel's 1933 musical comedy *Viktor und Viktoria* was the source for the 1982 movie *Victor/Victoria*, starring Broadway veterans

Singin' in the Rain (1952) with Gene Kelly.

GENE KELLY
DONALD O'CONNOR
DEBBIE REYNOLDS

Maurice Chevalier was one of Hollywood's first talkie stars. Showcase photo for Ernst Lubitsch's film operetta *The Love Parade*.

was recorded simultaneously with the picture; the process of synchronizing audio and video was not developed until some years later. Many early sound films look quite static, especially since—as is typical for enthusiastic use of any new technology—they were often overloaded with dialogue. Some progress came, however, when producer Rouben Mamoulian moved from Broadway to Hollywood and, with the 1929 movie *Applause*, developed a flowing and rhythmic narrative style.

Like Mamoulian, many theater performers, composers, writers, and producers made the move to movies. Jerome Kern and Irving Berlin spent several years in Hollywood, while Richard Rodgers and his partner Lorenz Hart only sojourned briefly amid the California motion-picture industry before returning to their preferred milieu, the Broadway theater. Other composers such as Harry Warren or Hoagy Carmichael first made their name through the movies. Successful operetta stars like Jeanette MacDonald and Nelson Eddy

Julie Andrews and Robert Preston. This movie in turn was refashioned into a Broadway show in 1996.

Since *The Jazz Singer* still contained some silent scenes, *The Broadway Melody of 1929* was touted as the first "all-talking, all-singing, all-dancing film." Many of these early movie musicals were set in the theatrical milieu as anchors for numerous song and dance numbers. The new technology was still plagued by certain problems: For one thing, while silent films had developed a sophisticated narrative style based on movable cameras, the camera for sound film had to be stationary since it was encased in a soundproof box to shut out the camera's own noise; this considerably limited the camera operator's mobility. In the early days, the sound

Fred Astaire was born May 10, 1899 as Frederick Austerlitz, and appeared on stage with his sister Adele from an early age. He first appeared on screen with Ginger Rogers in 1933. The sensational success of their dance number "The Carioca" in *Flying Down to Rio* (1933) launched a series of signal musicals of the 1930s. The films of Astaire and Rogers are distinguished by the team's accomplished style, and particularly by the ingenuity of the choreography, for which Astaire collaborated with Hermes Pan.

continued their careers on screen, as did Maurice Chevalier, who appeared as Danilo in Ernst Lubitsch's elegant and frivolous film version of Franz Léhar's *The Merry Widow*. The early Hollywood musicals were often based on the lightweight Broadway musical comedies of the 1920s, thanks in part to performers like Fred Astaire and Ginger Rogers.

Almost all successful stage musicals, beginning with *Show Boat* (filmed in 1929) through *Oklahoma!* (1955) to *Evita* (1996), have been adapted for the screen (though a significant number have not, or not yet). Many important works of the genre are known to the wider public both within the United States and abroad only through movie versions. Movie producers took great license in transforming shows from stage to screen: Plots were rewritten completely and original scoring replaced by supposedly more appealing songs by other composers. The 1949 movie version of Leonard Bernstein, Adolph Green, and Betty Comden's *On the Town* retained only the first three musical numbers from the 1944 stage show; the rest were composed for the movie by Roger Eden.

It was inevitable, perhaps, that Hollywood would not rest contented with adapting Broadway hits but would begin to generate

Powerful colors: A scene from the movie version of Rodgers and Hammerstein's *Carousel*.

musicals on its own. Very quickly, movie musicals were made from original scripts like *42nd Street* (1933), with music by Harry Warren, *Singin' in the Rain*, or Cole Porter's *High Society*; and many made the reverse voyage, from screen to stage.

42nd Street tells the classic story of a chorus girl who stands in for an ailing star and becomes a sensation herself. Busby Berkeley, who began his career in the *Ziegfeld Follies*, invented the new

A typical bird's eye still shot from Busby Berkeley's *Footlight Parade* (1933).

style of rousing cinematic choreography. In the 1930s, as a producer and choreographer, Berkeley created an independent aesthetic for cinematic musicals. His extremely movable camera, often filming from a bird's eye view, recorded hundreds of long-legged and scantily clad girls, as parts of a constantly changing design or pattern.

With Bing Crosby, Deanna Durbin, and Judy Garland, Hollywood produced its own musical stars, who had no theatrical stage

career either before or after they became movie stars. In the 1940's and 1950s, the former songwriter Arthur Freed produced a series of more intelligent and tasteful movie musicals for Metro-Goldwyn-Mayer, which distinguished themselves pleasantly from the corny and motley adaptations of large stage successes like *Oklahoma!* or *Carousel*. Both these musicals had been produced on Broadway by Rouben Mamoulian, but Mamoulian now joined the ranks of the successful team of

Stanley Donen and Gene Kelly as well as former stage impresario Vincente Minelli as producers actively working for Freed. Known for his skillful sense of color and careful work with actors, Minelli turned out some of the most beautiful musicals of the 1940s, including *Meet Me in St. Louis*, with his wife Judy Garland, and *An American in Paris* with the music of George Gershwin. Highlights from these MGM musicals were assembled for two retrospective compilations called *That's Entertainment*, the first directed by Jack Haley, Jr. (son of Garland's costar in the classic MGM musical *The Wizard of Oz*), the second by Gene Kelly.

In the 1950s, movie musicals seemed to go out of fashion. Of course, the biggest Broadway hits like *My Fair Lady* and *West Side Story* were made into movies, but original musicals like Walt Disney's *Mary Poppins* were relatively rare. The early 1970s actually saw one of the most critically acclaimed musical adaptations, Bob Fosse's dramatic adaptation of *Cabaret*, with Liza Minelli and Joel Grey (both of whom won Oscars for their performances). The 1980s brought Richard Attenborough's film version of *A Chorus Line*, but movie musicals have generally been few and far between. Some, like the film versions of the Off-Broadway productions *The Rocky Horror Show* (1973, filmed 1975) and *Grease* (1972, filmed in 1978 starring a young John Travolta and Australian pop singer Olivia Newton John), attained something of a cult status with a young audience. Since Alan Parker's *Fame* (1980), the genre of the movie musical has steadily declined, broken only in 1996 when Webber

Vincente Minelli's *An American in Paris* took a stylistic cue from the impressionistic colors of August Renoir's paintings.

Some of the Walt Disney Studios' animated musicals were subsequently reincarnated as theater productions, including *Beauty and the Beast* and the classic *Jungle Book*.

and Rice's much-ballyhooed *Evita* starring pop star Madonna drew audiences into movie theaters. On the other hand, recent musicals have been based on feature films, such as Andrew Lloyd Webber's *Sunset Boulevard*, based on the Billy Wilder melodrama of the same name, or Maury Yeston's *Nine*, based on on Federico Fellini's autobiographical film *8½*.

Now, near the end of the 20th century, the movie musical is something of an endangered species. In part, this may reflect the growing market for touring productions of popular shows undercutting into the financial potential of films while offering a different, unique, live experience. Many producers do not want the long-running stage musicals threatened by competition from film versions. This may be one reason why it

took 18 years for *Evita* to come to the screen; other reasons may have to do with a dramatic and aesthetic incongruence between the operatic and episodic shows now sweeping Broadway and the tastes of the movie-going public.

Among the most original film musicals are Jacques Demy's *Les Parapluies de Cherbourg* and *Les Demoiselles de Rochefort* (here with Catherine Deneuve and Françoise Dorléac), with dialogue sung to the music of Michel Legrand.

1929 – 1943

1929: Black Friday

The stock market crash and the Great Depression sobered the big, freewheeling party of the jazz age. The hangover was harsh, and the entertainment industry was hit especially hard. With the massive unemployment, most people—the general public on which Broadway depended—could no longer afford theater tickets. Movies with sound, especially musicals, offered a reasonably affordable alternative. In the 1927/28 season, Broadway saw a record 264 new productions. In 1935/36, at the peak of the Depression, there were only 138 openings. Between 1930 and 1940, 24 of an original 68 Broadway theaters closed; some were converted into movie theaters.

To many, the unconstrained cheer and carefree tone of musical comedies was well-suited enough to the optimism of the 1920s but inappropriate to the conditions of the Depression. In the early 1930s, sharper tones were heard on Broadway. Broadway responded to the competition coming from movies and radio and the taste of the public with biting satires on politics and current events, revealing a previously unknown social consciousness for the musical. Near the end of the decade, the genre matured musically and thematically with works by Gershwin, Rodgers and Hart, and the two Broadway newcomers Cole Porter and Kurt Weill. With their polished song lyrics, Porter and Hart set new standards.

Jokes, satire, irony, and deeper meaning

If the musical had always been a reflection of prevailing tastes, the sharp-tongued revues and comedies of the 1930s were a direct reaction to current political events. In 1930, George and Ira Gershwin, with authors Morrie Ryskind

and George S. Kaufman, successfully produced their failed 1927 satire on militarism and capitalism, *Strike Up the Band*, n a new and revised form on Broadway ironically, it was the revised version that oftened the original bite of the satire). The how describes the dream of an insatiable chocolate manufacturer, who drives the United States into war against Switzerland in order to monopolize the candy market, and who quickly changes his politics as necessary to stay in business. Song titles like "A Typical Self-Made American" or "Yankee Doodle Rhythm" were direct expressions of the four authors' ironic and antinationalistic stance. The next year the same team exceeded this success with a biting caricature of American politics. In the tradition of Gilbert and Sullivan's satirical operettas, *Of Thee I Sing* deals with an American presidential campaign. Ira Gershwin, George S. Kaufman, and Morrie Ryskind were honored with the prestigious Pulitzer Prize for their book and lyrics, marking the first time the Pulitzer was awarded to a musical. George Gershwin, as composer, was unnamed in the literary award, but his music made *Of Thee I Sing* the Gershwin brothers' greatest Broadway triumph; it ran for 441 performances. Theater critic George Jean Nathan hailed *Of Thee I Sing* as "the happiest and most successful native music-stage lampoon that has thus far come the way of the American theatre." The central characters, the bumbling future president John P. Wintergreen and his incompetent running mate Alexander Throttlebottom, also appear in the middle of *Let 'Em Eat Cake*. Although George Gershwin's music to *Let 'Em Eat Cake*

In *Of Thee I Sing* (1931), the presidential candidate Wintergreen promises to marry the winner of a beauty competition if he wins. When elected, however, he marries his secretary because she bakes such good rolls. Wintergreen escapes the displeasure of the people and diplomatic complications with France—the deserted beauty queen is a descendant of Napoleon—through his wife's pregnancy and the wedding of Vice President Throttlebottom with Miss America: The people and the French are reconciled.

1929 - 1943

Let 'Em Eat Cake, a sequel, warns of fascism as the possible consequence of the Depression's mass unemployment. Wintergreen, who has been voted out of office, sets up a dictatorship and wants to execute his former comrade-in-arms Throttlebottom.

In Rodgers and Hart's *I'd Rather Be Right*, author George S. Kaufman brought the real president Franklin D. Roosevelt, portrayed by Broadway veteran George M. Cohan, onstage to say: "What this country suffers from, is, that I, its chief, have no idea what it suffers from." Richard Rodgers, like Cohan, was a vehement opponent of Roosevelt's politics and the New Deal, and Lorenz Hart furnished the sharply ironic lyrics.

1929 – 1943

was his most mature work to date, the story dealt with impending fascism and failed with the public.

Another of George and Ira Gershwin's hits during this period was *Girl Crazy*, which opened on Broadway on October 14, 1930. The musical comedy, containing one of Gershwin's most popular hit songs, "I Got Rhythm", starred the then only 19-year-old Ginger Rodgers. Set on a godforsaken farm in Arizona, the story tells how the playboy heir, Danny, transforms his bleak inheritance into an amusement farm for weary city-dwellers. *Girl Crazy* has been filmed three times, most notably in 1943 with Judy Garland and Mickey Rooney in the title roles.

Irving Berlin always had a sure feel for the zeitgeist. In the 1920s, he satisfied popular taste with his luxuriously produced Music Box revues, during the First and Second World Wars he wrote the successful patriotic shows *Yip, Yip, Yaphank* (1918) and *This Is the Army* (1943), in which he appeared personally. In 1933, he composed the songs to *As Thousands Cheer*, a revue in which the musical numbers and sketches corresponded to the diverse departments of a daily newspaper: Juxtaposed with a musical weather forecast was a sketch about Josephine Baker, who despite her fame and wealth was longing for Harlem ("Harlem on My Mind"); other famous targets of parodies or homage were Mahatma Ghandi, John D. Rockefeller, and the Statue of Liberty. The most serious scene was based on an actual headline "Unknown Negro Lynched by Angry Mob": Ethel Walters played a mother who has to explain to her children at suppertime that their father has been murdered by racists and will never come home again.

Needle jabs

Late 1937 brought one of the most sensational successes Broadway had ever seen. The leftist International Ladies Garment Workers' Union commissioned architect and amateur musician Harold Rome to compose the music for a revue for amateur performers. The sketches were written by five different authors, all of them amateurs. On November 27, 1937 the first performance of *Pins and Needles* arrived on the stage. One of Rome's song texts could well serve as the motto for all the political satire musical productions of the age: "Sing me a Song of Social Significance / All Other Tunes Are Taboo." Contrary to expectations, the amateur production of *Pins and Needles* was neither dry nor preachy, but full of jokes, acerbity, and self-mockery. With 1,108 performances, the amateur playgroup of the ILGWU became, for a short period, the longest-running show on Broadway (albeit in theaters with very limited seating capacity). With *Pins and Needles*, Harold Rome began a long career as a song and musical composer. At first he continued to draw upon themes of social criticism and was successful in 1954 with *Fanny*, an adaptation of Marcel Pagnol's Southern French folk theater trilogy *Marius*, an almost operatic work of extraordinary musical wealth.

In the summer before *Pins and Needles* was produced, one of its authors, Marc Blitzstein, wanted to produce a musical parable about the conflict between industrial capitalists and steelworkers entitled *The Cradle Will Rock*. Both the actors' and the musicians' unions considered the work communist and forbade their members from performing in it. A court injunction stalled the opening at literally the last minute on June 16,

Pins and Needles: The two "angels of freedom" Hitler and Stalin in Harold Rome's satirical revue. The revue was constantly updated with revised songs and sketches that targeted the international imperialism of Hitler, Mussolini, Hirohito, and later also Stalin ("Four Little Angels of Peace"), the dangers of unregulated capitalism ("Doing the Reactionary"), the advantages of a unionized work force ("It's Better With a Union Man"), or a leisurely Sunday in Central Park ("Sunday in the Park").

Marc Blitzstein accompanies his work *The Cradle Will Rock* at the piano.

1937. The producer, however, a 22-year-old named Orson Welles who had already made a name with his theater and radio productions, and his Mercury Theatre colleague John Houseman would not be deterred and rented another theater the same evening where they presented an improvised performance: Marc Blitzstein sat alone onstage at the piano, and the performers whose unions had forbidden them from taking the stage performed in the aisles.

The American Folk Opera

When George Gershwin attended a reading of Du Bose Heyward's novel *Porgy* in 1926, he immediately saw its operatic possibilities. Oscar Hammerstein and Jerome Kern's *Show Boat* had confirmed his conviction that the musical theater could tackle serious subjects. He did not yet feel accomplished enough as a composer to take on such an ambitious project, and, moreover, because the novel was being dramatized by Dorothy and Dubose Heyward into a play, the rights to the novel were not available. Finally, eight years later, after he had written the demanding scores of *Strike Up the Band* and *Of Thee I Sing*, Gershwin felt ready to tackle the project.

In 1976, the Houston Grand Opera mounted an unabridged production of *Porgy and Bess* on Broadway.

The novel *Porgy* and the play of the same name outline episodes of life in a black ghetto in Charleston, South Carolina, around 1930. Gershwin's *Porgy and Bess* moves the love of the crippled Porgy and Bess, a lovely but weak-willed woman, to the center of the action, while retaining the rich milieu. Du Bose Heyward wrote the book and, with Ira Gershwin, the lyrics. So both authors and the composer studied ghetto life in South Carolina. Its slang and its music—spirituals, blues, jazz—served as raw material for Gershwin's score. Heyward had spoken of black music as the expression of that which cannot be said. Gershwin combined this emotional quality with polished musical knowhow, creating recitatives and leitmotifs out of blue notes and syncopated rhythms for an extraordinary musical drama. He spent eleven months composing and an additional nine months orchestrating the piece. The Metropolitan Opera offered to produce the premiere, billing *Porgy and Bess* as the "American Folk Opera," but Gershwin declined: He insisted on casting black singers and performers, knowing that the Met would have inevitably used a white ensemble in blackface. So *Porgy and Bess* opened on October 10, 1935 at the Alvin Theatre on Broadway.

Porgy and Bess: Todd Duncan (Porgy), Ann Brown (Bess), and John W. Bubbles (Sportin' Life) in the premiere of Gershwin's folk opera.

1929 - 1943

At a concert (unstaged) tryout in Carnegie Hall, the show ran four hours. During the final rehearsals and tryouts in Boston, extensive cuts to the score were made. Concerning the process of trimming the piece down to an acceptable Broadway length, his friends and colleagues, including the show's producer Rouben Mamoulian and his friend, fellow composer Alexander Steinert, observed about Gershwin, "Very few composers, if any, would have stood by and witnessed with comparative calm the dismemberment of their brain-child until it had been reduced by nearly a quarter! He was quite philosophical about it." And Mamoulian explained, "His theater sense was so keen that, no matter how much he loved a musical motive or an aria, he would not hesitate to cut it if it improved the work as a whole."

Acclaimed in Boston, Porgy and Bess received only conditional approval of the New

York critics when it opened on Broadway. Serious music journalists had already written about Gershwin's hybrid work. Critics quibbled over whether the work was an opera or a musical. To arguments that, with "Summertime," "I Got Plenty of Nuttin'," and other songs, *Porgy and Bess* had too many hit songs to be an opera, Gershwin replied in an article in the *New York Times* that "Many of the most successful operas of the past have had songs. Nearly all of Verdi's operas contain what are known as 'song hits.' *Carmen* is almost a collection of song hits." The original production of *Porgy and Bess* ran for 124 performances, impressive for an opera, but not so for a Broadway show. It quickly found its way, however, into international opera houses and has been successfully revived on Broadway several times. Gershwin's notion of an "American folk opera" would be developed later by other composers including Kurt Weill and Leonard Bernstein. After *Porgy*, Gershwin worked in Hollywood, writing songs for movies, including "They Can't Take That Away from Me" for Fred Astaire, and planned a musical theater adaptation of the Jewish Dibbuk legend. His death on July 11, 1938 from a brain tumor tragically ended the breathtaking development of this great American composer.

With *The Threepenny Opera* (based on John Gay's *Beggar's Opera*) and *Happy End* (inspired by Damon Runyon's Broadway stories), Kurt Weill and Bertolt Brecht developed a musical theater form in pre-1933 Berlin that strongly resembled the American musical.

Kurt Weill

Kurt Weill came to musicals from a different direction. Born in 1900 in Dessau, Germany, the son of a choirmaster, Weill studied composition in Berlin with both Engelbert Humperdinck and Ferruccio Busoni. Under the influence of the latter, Weill seemed for a time to develop in the direction of the expressionist composers of the time; in 1922, his twelve-tone music for a children's ballet called *Magic Night* hopelessly overtaxed his young public. However, by 1925 he had discovered his talent for stage compositions, and wrote his first opera in collaboration with Georg Kaiser. In 1927, Weill then made made the acquaintance of Bertolt Brecht, the German poet/playwright, together with whom he produced a masterly synthesis of jazz and pop music with traditional forms in *The Threepenny Opera* (1929), based on John Gay's *Beggar's Opera*, and *Happy End* (1929). The Nazis were no more enchanted by his "Negro music" than they were by his Jewish background, and Weill was forced to flee the Nazis in 1933. From France, where he wrote the dance theater piece *The Seven Deadly Sins* for choreographer George Balanchine, he came in 1935 to New York. In New York, he was deeply moved by a tryout performance of *Porgy and Bess*. He resolved never again to speak the language of his homeland, from which he had been expelled, and to devote himself to writing American musical theater. His first attempt, the antiwar parable *Johnny Johnson* (1936), which was produced by the leftist Group Theatre, suffered from a naive libretto and, despite direction by the legendary acting teacher Lee Strasberg, and Weill's much-praised music, was not a success. Two years later, with dramatist Maxwell Anderson, Weill tried again: *Knickerbocker Holiday* comments on fascist tendencies in the United States by telling of the supposedly historical conflict between the dictatorial governor of New Amsterdam, Peter Stuyvesant, and the revolutionary free spirit and American pioneer Brom Broeck. These two characters not only have different political

Ginger Rogers on the psychiatrist's couch in the movie of *Lady in the Dark*, which Weill did not particularly like.

The premise for *Knickerbocker Holiday* was Washington Irving's anonymously published 1809 Diedrich Knickerbocker's humorous *History of New York*. "Knickerbocker" became a nickname for the New York population. The originally Dutch colony Nieuw Amsterdam was conquered in 1664 during Stuyvesant's administration by the English and renamed New York.

1929 – 1943

The "circus dream sequence" from Kurt Weill's *Lady in the Dark*, with Danny Kaye in the middle.

Weill's greatest success on Broadway was the 1943 comedy *One Touch of Venus*, with lyrics by Ogden Nash and book by Nash and S. J.

Perelman. A Venus statue, roused to life, pursues the barber Rodney Hatch. Rodney jumps out of the frying pan into the fire: At first, he does not want to free the love-besotted Venus, then his fiancée Gloria and her mother cause a scene. The police accuse him of murdering Gloria, who has been spirited away by Venus to the North Pole, and when Rodney finally decides to woo Venus, she wants nothing more to do with him and returns to the museum. There Rodney, deserted in the meantime by Gloria as well, at last meets a potential wife on his way out of the art school where Venus is housed.

world views but are also both in love with the innkeeper's daughter Tina. The show is filled with allusions to current events and real personalities, through which Anderson also attacked President Franklin Roosevelt. Weill's acidic-lyrical ballad "September Song," sung yearningly by Walter Huston as Stuyvesant, revealed glimpses of the aggressive display of a would-be dictator.

Lady in the Dark, in 1941, dealt with psychoanalysis. The author Moss Hart originally wanted to write a play, but the material was modified by Weill and Ira Gershwin into a musical. At the center of the story is the successful fashion editor Liza Elliott, who suffers mental "disturbances." Torn between three men, she comes to a simple resolution of the conflict with the help of interpretation of dreams. A decisive role is played by a fragment of melody, which is carried through the piece like a leitmotif. In the end Liza chooses the man who successfully completes the lost song, "My Ship," which stands for Liza's psychological healing. All the other musical numbers are reserved for three dream sequences, reflecting Liza's fears and longings. Weill spoke of three mini operas, which carried the action of the play musically. With the tongue-twisting song "Tschaikowsky," in which lyricist Ira Gershwin immortalized the names of many Russian composers, comedian Danny Kaye became a popular favorite.

Kurt Weill kept his eye on the goal of composing an "American opera" that would appeal to a broad audience while integrating drama and music into a unified whole. In the 1929 play *Street Scene* by Elmer Rice, Weill believed he had found the appropriate vehicle to follow in the steps of Gershwin's *Porgy and Bess*. With Rice and poet Langston Hughes,

Weill undertook the project. The musical drama *Street Scene* (1947) describes a day in the life of the residents of a New York tenement, telling of their sorrows and small delights. Normal events like the birth of a baby, neighbors gossiping over trivia, or the happy greeting of the ice vendor on a hot summer day are overshadowed by the violent argument of a married couple. The consistent naturalism of plot, action, dialogue, and setting contrasts with the musical score, in which Weill employed the breadth of musical means of expression: Songs, arias, duets, ensembles, and orchestral interludes. Weill's theater music interweaves modern and traditional, American and European stylistic devices. The following year's *Love Life* was an unorthodox—though also, according to the librettist Alan Jay Lerner, half-baked—mixture. The fantastical story of a never-aging married couple, which spanned from 1791 to the mid-20th century, describes in vaudeville style the changes in the man-woman relationship over time. The songs are not embedded in the action but, in the tradition of Weill's former collaborator, Bertolt Brecht, comment upon it.

In 1949's *Lost in the Stars*, Weill teamed up again with Maxwell Anderson to treat the inhumanity of the South African system of apartheid. Where his music for *Love Life* had been truer to the traditions of musical comedy, Weill now returned to the operatic idiom for this drama of a black pastor whose son becomes a criminal under the conditions of racial segregation. Todd Duncan, who had played Porgy, took the leading role.

To Weill's delight, the Broadway audience accepted his demanding musical tragedy with its solemn songs and powerful hymns. The material to which Weill and Anderson turned

The 1947 neorealist music drama *Street Scene* in its original Broadway production.

1929 – 1943

A 1995 coproduction of *Street Scene* by the Houston Grand Opera and the Berlin Theater of the West.

In 1934, with *Anything Goes*, Cole Porter celebrated his greatest success to date. The book, by Kern and Gershwin's former comrades Guy Bolton and P. G. Wodehouse, is set on board a luxury liner sailing from New York to London. The two Britons made sure that the banal plot was sufficiently amusing and offered opportunities for some of Porter's best songs, including "I Get a Kick Out of You," "You're the Top," or the title song.

1929 – 1943

next appeared to offer all the requirements for a popular American musical theater piece: *Huckleberry Finn*. Weill had already composed several songs, when he suddenly died of a heart attack on March 19, 1950.

With his coauthors, Kurt Weill had proven that the musical theater could handle dramatic and tragic subjects and could carry a message. The influence of his music cannot be overestimated. Weill became the model for a whole generation of composers who emulated his combining of popular, entertaining music theater with ambitious musical forms.

Cole Porter: The art of the song writer

Just as Kurt Weill gave the musical new musical means of expression and opened it to demanding subjects, Cole Porter, born in 1891 in the tiny Midwestern town of Peru, Indiana, perfected the art of song writing. Porter flirted with being a composer, a "professional amateur." His grandfather had made an enormous fortune selling wood and coal, so his grandson Cole was already a millionaire when he began, as the old gentleman wished, to study law at Yale. Porter wrote his first songs for amateur shows at college, including the Yale Bulldog song. He convinced his grandfather to allow him to study music at Harvard. Unlike composers who came from less affluent families—some utterly poor, some middle-class or more prosperous—Berlin, Gershwin, Kern and Rodgers, who were all enthusiasts for music and theater at a young age, Porter never considered composing to be a profession or a calling. He had an extraordinary talent for song writing, but his wealth meant he would never have to work for a living. Unlike his assimilation-conscious Jewish colleagues, who wanted to create an

American music, the midwestern Porter presented himself as cosmopolitan. He enjoyed his life among the upper ten thousand of the old and new world, and threw parties in his Venetian Palazzo Rezzonico, or in a suite at the Waldorf-Astoria, that rivaled anything in *The Great Gatsby*.

By 1916 Porter had composed the music to a Broadway show, the "patriotic comic opera" *See America First*. It was a huge flop. Apparently unfazed by the failure, Porter proceeded to Europe and joined the French Foreign Legion. He spent the 1920s predominantly as an expatriot in Paris, only occasionally writing a number for a revue producer whom he met on a cruise. In 1928 Porter returned to Broadway with the musical comedy *Paris*. Although the piece was a lightweight, as were most productions of the time, Porter caused a sensation with frivolous songs, including his first bona fide hit, "Let's Do It."

Everything Porter did was marked by his own unmistakable style. As a composer and song writer, Porter continually polished the words and melody until he produced glittering and immaculate masterpieces that expressed his subtle wit and exquisite taste. Since, as author, Porter already knew when writing the lines what he, as composer, intended (and vice versa), he was successful again and again at inventing extraordinary rhyme schemes and surprising turns. His allusion-packed lyrics, full of alliteration, internal rhyme, and onomatopoeic punning, also achieved a high level of musicality. Because Porter's melodies, which often shift between major and minor keys, contain daring rhythms and are so apparently inseparable from the text, Porter is hard to translate. Even the

1929 – 1943

Anything Goes carried on the tradition of the light musical comedies of the 1920s. The plot originally revolved around a shipwreck, but the coincidence of an actual ship disaster prompted the producer to hire two new writers shortly before the opening to rework the story. These changes contributed to the superficiality of the nonetheless charming piece. Scene photo from a London performance, 1989.

Alliteration à la Cole Porter:
(from "It's De-Lovely")
It's delightful,
It's delicious,
It's delectable,
It's delirious,
It's dilemma,
It's delimit,
It's deluxe,
It's de-lovely.

Internal rhyme
(from "In The Still of the Night")
Or will this dream of mine
Fade out of sight,
Like the morning growing dim
On the rim of the hill
In the chill still of the night?

(from "Anything Goes")
Good Authors too who
Once knew better words
Now only use four-letter
words
Writing prose
Anything goes!

In Cole Porter's *Dubarry Was a Lady* (1939), the rest room attendant of a night club, played by Bert Lahr, dreams he is Ludwig XIV. The leg he is inspecting belongs to Betty Grable.

seemingly simplest of lyrics have a certain ineffable, untranslatable Porter touch: "Flying too high with some guy in the sky is my idea of nothing to do, yet I get a kick out of you." His compositions usually offer, instead of invariably equal repetitions of verse and refrain, carefully worked out variations on the original theme. The primary emotional style of his characters is an ironic reserve that lies mainly in the lyrics, which reflect Porter's own ironical temperament. Porter's protagonists tend to meet their emotional confusions, their triumphs, and small defeats with a smile and a joke on their lips, and Porter held the conviction that it was better to laugh in a palace than weep in a hut.

In contrast to Gershwin, Weill, or Rodgers and Hart, the apolitical Porter fostered no ambition to pack serious themes—to say nothing of messages—into his works. The comedies for which he wrote his songs offered light entertainment and harkened back unabashedly to the musical comedies of the 1920s.

While Porter managed to be untouched by the Great Depression, in 1937 he encountered tragedy at first hand: His legs were

nearly destroyed in a riding accident and until his death he suffered constant pain and was occasionally dependent on a wheelchair. To avoid amputation, he underwent 31 operations, though with little ultimate success at restoring his health or mobility. Outwardly, though, Cole Porter was always Cole Porter, the cheerful bon vivant. He had no desire to be a part of the lengthy rehearsal process for a show and usually delivered his songs to his producer and went off to Paris or on a cruise through the South Seas. He cheerfully explained that he had no knack for writing librettos. Because of his lack of interest in drama, many of his songs are at best, thinly, integrated into the story of the early comedies. Alternately, the plots are sometimes stretched incredibly to accommodate his songs, though this hardly seems to matter. In 1948 Porter for the first time undertook to write effective theater music; the result was *Kiss Me, Kate*.

Rodgers and Hart

Like Kurt Weill, Richard Rodgers and Lorenz Hart were exploring new materials, themes, and forms for the musical. With the 1926 production of *Peggy Ann*, cowritten with Herbert Fields, they took psychoanalysis as the subject of musical comedy, fifteen years before Weill's *Lady in the Dark*. Their adaptation of Mark Twain, *A Connecticut Yankee*, opened on Broadway a month before Jerome Kern's pioneering *Show Boat*. In 24 years, they wrote 29 musicals. Like Cole Porter, Hart repeatedly reinvented song writing. His lyrics for *A Connecticut Yankee* derived their comic effects from the clash of Old English and contemporary American slang. Unlike most songwriters of his time, Hart chose to treat his audience with intelligence. In 1931, Rodgers and Hart's *America's Sweetheart* was a highly successful Hollywood satire, but not long after, they themselves were enticed out to the movie capital. In Rouben Mamoulian's *Love Me Tonight*, Maurice Chevalier sings one of their best-known melodies, "Isn't It Romantic?" Richard Rodgers, however, had been in love with the theater since childhood,

Despite his physical disability after a riding accident, Cole Porter always appeared neat as a pin at Broadway premieres. Porter, in true cavalier form, claims that he worked on the text of his song "At Long Last Love" while waiting for help after the horse fell on him.

1929 – 1943

Rodgers and Hart's extravaganza *Jumbo* was made into a movie in 1962 with Jimmy Durante, who had also appeared in the show on Broadway.

1929 – 1943

A performance of *On Your Toes* with the Stuttgart Ballet in 1992 ...

... and in the New York premiere in 1936: Ray Bolger dances for his life in the dramatic ballet "Slaughter on Tenth Avenue."

and Lorenz Hart also missed the atmosphere of Broadway. They celebrated their return to New York in 1935 with a costly extravaganza called *Jumbo*. This Romeo and Juliet story of the children of two competing ringmasters allowed them to use circus attractions with performers, clowns, and animal trainers. The production was staged in the gigantic Hippodrome, which was torn down after *Jumbo*'s run. With each of their following productions, Rodgers and Hart broke new ground. The 1936 dance musical *On Your Toes* merged the worlds of vaudeville, gangsters, and classic and modern ballet, and included an extended dance sequence, choreographed by George Balanchine, as a dramatic device. The action reaches a peak in the jazz ballet "Slaughter on Tenth Avenue," in which the protagonist literally dances to save his life: A mob hitman is after him, and he prolongs the crescendo of the finale, in which a deadly shot will ring out, long enough for

the killer to be apprehended. *On Your Toes* was a breakthrough not only for Balanchine, but for the dancer and leading actor Ray Bolger (remembered today primarily for his role of the Cowardly Lion in *The Wizard of Oz*).

In *Babes in Arms* (1937), the children of vaudeville performers prove that they can put on a show, just like their ever-touring parents. The show introduced two great Rodgers and Hart hits: "My Funny Valentine" and "The Lady Is a Tramp." In the same year

(1927), *I'd Rather Be Right* satirized the politics of Franklin D. Roosevelt. For *The Boys from Syracuse* (1938), Rodgers and Hart dug up an author who is still often mined for the raw material of musicals: Shakespeare. Their adaptation of his *Comedy of Errors* is a raucous farce about two sets of twins, separated at birth. Identical brothers, both named Antipholus with their identical-twin servants, likewise both

named Dromio, cause consternation, especially since they are themselves unaware of their doubles' existence. The misunderstanding is only cleared up when the father of both Antipholi arrives (in naturalistic *deus ex machina* fashion). Lorenz Hart's brother Teddy played one of the two Dromios; the other was played by Jimmy Savo, a comedian with whom Teddy Hart was frequently confused.

The Boys from Syracuse was the first musical based on a play by William Shakespeare. Jimmy Savo as Dromio from Syracuse in the original 1938 production.

1929 – 1943

With *Pal Joey* (1940), Rodgers and Hart struck new chords. The title character Joey is a weak and corrupt gigolo who works in a shabby night club in Chicago. This was the first musical with an antihero at the center of the story. Caught between two women, Joey chooses the older, richer, and married Vera Simpson. Vera uses her husband's money to buy Joey his own club. He, on the other hand, remains constantly on the make and eventually his selfishness becomes apparent even to Vera. In *Lady, Be Good!* (1924) the hero courted by two women chooses love over money, and gets both. In 1940, Pal Joey stands empty-handed at the end. The humor in the show does not shrink from cynicism, corruption, and a greed- and sex- charged atmosphere. Rodgers's music varies from the sounds of operetta with soft ballads to hard urban jazz. Hart's lyrics are full of sarcasm and erotic allusion.

In the song "Zip!" a striptease dancer reports that when practicing her trade—Zip!—she muses on Schopenhauer. For the character of the rich and cynical Vera Simpson, Rodgers and Hart

wrote the lovely ballad "Bewitched, Bothered and Bewildered," which reflects all the shades of being in love: Unsentimental and self-ironically, Vera marvels at her own feelings for the good-for-nothing Joey, speaks openly of their sexual excitement, of the simultaneous, almost childlike enchantment, but also of his intention to remain financially dependent on her. The music follows Hart's lyrics in its turns of sentiment to caustic sarcasm, from heated pleasure to cool calculation. *Pal Joey*'s realism is reminiscent of Hollywood's film noir genre of the 1940s, which painted a comparably dismal picture of American society.

By Jupiter, produced in 1942, was the most successful of all Rodgers and Hart musicals to date. In this story, the women of the mythical kingdom of Pontus overthrow their husbands' rule and establish an Amazon state. Only the Greeks under the leadership of Theseus and Hercules can restore the

1929 – 1943

Looking at Gene Kelly as "Pal Joey," it is hard to believe that he played the first musical antihero. This role made Kelly a star, while his costar, Vivienne Segal, was already celebrated on Broadway at the beginning of the century.

patriarchy. The work on *By Jupiter* had been haunted by Lorenz Hart's increasing drinking problems and unstable health. The solid, disciplined, happily married Rodgers and the genial, Bohemian Hart had been opposites from the beginning as partners and friends. Hart turned down Rodgers' suggestion that they base their next musical on the 1931 play *Green Grow the Lilacs*. Hart withdrew on an extended vacation in Mexico, so Rodgers for the first time since 1919 collaborated with a lyricist other than Hart. On March 31, 1943, the first musical by Rodgers and Hammerstein opened. It was called *Oklahoma!* and marked the beginning of the most successful partnership in the history of the musical. Rodgers only worked with his longtime friend Lorenz Hart once more: In November 1943 a revival of *A Connecticut Yankee* opened, refurbished and with new songs. At the opening, Hart suddenly disappeared. A couple of days later he was found dead of pneumonia in a New York hotel room.

1929 – 1943

Frank Sinatra and Rita Hayworth in the movie version of *Pal Joey* (1957).

1943 – 1957

Changing times

After the Japanese air attack on the U.S. Pacific Fleet at Pearl Harbor on December 7, 1942, the United States entered World War II on the side of the Allies. Victory in Europe and the Pacific brought new changes, as inevitably reflected by the popular culture. The musical satires of the 1930s had been unsparing in their political criticism, but these voices were muffled somewhat under FDR's efforts to unify the sentiments of the nation and the resources of the economy. Immediately after the defeat of the Germans and the Japanese, a new war brought with it a change in values. This was the Cold War. The ideological and economic conflict with the Soviet Union, newly elevated to superpower status, ushered in a conservative era in the United States. The reactionary Senator Joseph McCarthy started his fight against "Un-American Activities" as a witchhunt against leftist intellectuals, who, he claimed were planning a communist overthrow of the U. S. government. The musical turned away from controversial politics toward more timeless and universal themes and worlds of melody. The shows of Richard Rodgers and Oscar Hammerstein mirror the tastes of the times and, through their earnest subjects, complex musical settings, and the quality of their dance, helped the genre gain acceptance as a legitimate art form. The musical play or drama supplanted the musical comedy. No materials, no subjects, no authors, from Homer to Voltaire to Truman Capote, from Shakespeare to Eugene O'Neill, were off-limits to musical authors as sources for stories or media for messages. Many composers replaced the simple song with forms based on classic musical theater. These general tendencies went hand in hand with stylistic variation, expressing the individual temperaments of composers and writers. The musical passed through romantic operetta-like works such as Rodgers and Hammerstein's *The King and I* and Lerner and Loewe's *My Fair Lady*, with classical musical comedies like Irving Berlin's *Annie Get Your Gun* and Cole Porter's *Kiss Me, Kate*, and shows like Frank Loesser's *Guys and Dolls* or Leonard Bernstein and Stephen Sondheim's *West Side Story*, which blended jazz with polished compostional techniques, in the heydey of the Broadway musical.

The Golden Apple (1954) with music by Jerome Moross and lyrics by John Latouche was an adaptation of Homer's Oydssey. For its illustrious plot, intelligent adaptation, and almost total abandonment of spoken dialogue, the work was praised by the critics but failed at the box office.

The Musical as a Unified Work

Rodgers and Hammerstein: *Oklahoma!*
In 1943, with their first collaborative effort, Richard Rodgers and Oscar Hammerstein became overnight the most successful team on Broadway. *Oklahoma!* ran for 2,248 successive performances and broke all standing records many times over. The successful team wrote other musicals in two-year intervals, most of which ran almost as long as their first. After the opening of *Oklahoma!* on March 31, 1943, their audience, critics, and colleagues declared unanimously that this show set new standards. Brooks Atkinson, drama critic for the *New York Times*, described it as a unified work of art in the Wagnerian mode, and Cole Porter laconically remarked that writing musical scores in the face of Rodgers and Hammerstein's achievement would be very hard work indeed.

That their first production as a team was celebrated as a milestone as important as

1943 – 1957

Oklahoma! influenced the development of the musical more than any other work of its genre. In 1953, the title song, performed here by the original cast, became the anthem for the state of Oklahoma.

> "When a show functions perfectly, then, it's because all the individual parts complement each other ... The orchestrations sound the way the costumes look."
> Richard Rodgers
>
> According to Oscar Hammerstein, it's not the "tangibles" that make the show work, it's the "spirit."

During the late 1940s and early 1950s, Richard Rodgers (left) and Oscar Hammerstein (right) reigned supreme on Broadway, like Andrew Lloyd Webber in the 1980s.

1943 – 1957

Show Boat conferred upon Rodgers and Hammerstein a certain contemporary and international reputation. Many of the innovations they introduced subsequently turned into conventions. Moreover, *Oklahoma!* was nothing absolutely new: *Porgy and Bess* and *Pal Joey* had already told serious stories, the ballet was already part of the story of *On Your Toes*, and dream sequences told via music and choreography were used by Kurt Weill in *Lady in the Dark*. *Oklahoma!* is nonetheless considered a style-setting and innovative musical because it took the integration of plot, music, and dance numbers a step farther. If *Show Boat* or *Porgy and Bess* were wondrous individual achievements without great followings, the productions of Rodgers and Hammerstein attracted a broader audience to the idea of the musical play.

Oklahoma! tells of rural life in an Indian territory at the beginning of the 20th century in the no-longer-so-Wild West. The pretty young Laurey stands between two men, the cheerful cowboy Curly and the sinister farm worker Jud. The rivalry of the two escalates through a competition over picnic baskets, prepared—to be auctioned off as a fundraiser—by the single ladies of the community. When Curly puts up his horse, saddle, and revolver to outbid Jud for Laurey's basket, Laurey finally decides in Curly's favor. On their wedding day, the fanatical Jud starts a fight and ends up falling on his own knife. He dies, and there are no impediments to Laurey and Curly's happiness. The Indian territory becomes one of the United States under the name Oklahoma.

Often, the author of a book or of the lyrics for a show are overshadowed by the composer. But when Richard Rodgers left his partnership with Lorenz Hart and began working with Oscar

Hammerstein, the author's influence on the music became evident. Rodgers' style changed in his collaboration with Hammerstein; it came nearer in orchestration and vocal expression to the sound of the operetta. The jazz influence heard in many Rodgers and Hart songs faded from Rodgers' later compositions, which contained hardly any offbeat syncopated rhythms. Hammerstein's good-spirited humor comes through in the reflective tone of *Oklahoma!*'s text, as Lorenz Hart's cosmopolitan and sarcastic wit was clear in Rodgers' earlier songs. Hammerstein's lyrics are consciously straightforward; their humor arises from situations and characters, not from the lyricist's inherent verbal wit. In the hands of a Lorenz Hart or a Cole Porter, a song like "I Can't Say No," in which a young woman declares her constitutional inability to refuse a man, might have been riddled with coquettish commentary and erotic allusion.

"Pore Jud is Dead!": The outsider Jud describes his own death in a macabre duet with Curly. Stage photo from a Broadway revival.

Much of *Oklahoma!*'s reputation rested on the long ballet sequence at the end the first act, choreographed by Agnes de Mille. The ballet sequence thenceforward

Indeed, Porter's song "Always True to You in My Fashion," from *Kiss Me, Kate*, is just this kind of number, and the tonal contrast between the two is obvious. Hammerstein presents the naive and sincere statement of a girl at a loss to explain her own behavior. The verses express emotion simply in the character's own words, with no self-conscious subtext. Rodgers' music grasps these inflections and emphasizes the earnestness of the characters' feelings. The skilled composer, who is known for writing songs quickly—"Oh,

became a virtual sine qua non for any ambitious musical production. In a dream presented in dance, Laurey has grave misgivings about the conflict between Curly and Jud. Where another musical would have sent the audience into the intermission with a cheerful, hummable tune, Rodgers and Hammerstein brought the tension to a peak with the foreshadowing of Curly's possible death.

1943 - 1957

George Bizet's 1875 opera *Carmen* was a model for both George Gershwin and Kurt Weill, who strived to write "American folk opera." Oscar Hammerstein americanized Bizet's original score in 1943 and produced it as *Carmen Jones.* Photo from the movie version with Dorothy Dandridge and Harry Belafonte.

What a Beautiful Morning" was supposedly written in ten minutes—had the control needed to make arduous art seem simple.

He focused his attention on the theatrical realism of his work. Characters are defined, not augmented or displayed, through songs: When Curly enters with his good-humored "Oh, What a Beautiful Morning," he is the counterpart for Jud, whose only song "Lonely Room" expresses his loneliness and frustration. The motifs of the twelve musical numbers of *Oklahoma!* return throughout the show. Individual songs, interspersed with dialogue, are reprised, tossed around to other characters, enlarged, varied. In this way, Rodgers and Hammerstein crafted a close relationship between the story and the music. Nevertheless, as full of character and emotion as these songs are, they do not really advance the plot. Nothing is substantially different at the end of the song itself, although the audience has a chance to experience the emotional currents through the song and dance. The dramatic moments in *Oklahoma!* are always expressed in dialogue, as in a play.

Oklahoma! stimulated other producers, composers, and authors to seek extraordinary subjects and more ambitious musical means. Rodgers and Hammerstein, however, would continue to dominate the musical theater in their time in a manner unmatched until the eventual ascendance of Andrew Lloyd Webber.

From *Carousel* to *The Sound of Music*
Rodgers and Hammerstein's following works were also clearly in the operetta tradition of musical theater (as opposed to the modern jazz tradition). Efforts toward a seriousness informed by a conservative outlook and

stamped by politically correct earnestness are reflected in Oscar Hammerstein's books. *Carousel*, which opened in 1945, was an adaptation of a play by Ferenc Molnar, *Liliom*, set in the outskirts of Budapest. Rodgers and Hammerstein moved the story to the coast of Maine in 1873. Molnar had refused to sell either Gershwin or Puccini the rights for a musical theater adaptation of his play, but after he saw *Oklahoma!*, he agreed to place his material into the hands of Rodgers and Hammerstein. The pessimistic end of the play was refashioned to sound a more hopeful note: the show ends with the powerful hymn "You'll Never Walk Alone," one of Rodgers' most beautiful melodies. In place of the standard overture, a potpourri of the musical numbers to come, the show begins with a ballet pantomime by the whole ensemble, for which Rodgers composed the expressive, lilting "Carousel Waltz." With Billy and Julie's duet "If I Loved You," Rodgers and Hammerstein again employed a musical-dramaturgical concept they had tested in *Oklahoma!*: In a single ten-minute sequence, they alternate song verses and spoken dialogue, showing the shifting interplay of approach and avoidance and of longing and mistrust between the two characters as they fall in love. The use of soliloquy, in the introspective monologue of

the expectant father Billy Bigelow, transcends the simple song form; here it created a

highly symphonic musical expression for the fluctuating feelings of the character, of his joy, anxiety, plans, and hopes for his child.

Carousel is a parable about human longing and weakness and the unavoidability of guilt. The naive young factory worker Julie gets pregant by her good-for-nothing beau, carnival barker Billy Bigelow. Billy is killed committing a

robbery. Fifteen years later his spirit is allowed to visit earth for a day, to accomplish a good deed. He anonymously visits his daughter Louise and gives her a small star, which he has secretly stolen. As she shrinks away from him, he feels guilty again and strikes her. However, the star will protect the lonely Louise in the future.

1943 – 1957

Carousel was one of the most impressive Broadway revivals of the 1990s, produced by Nicholas Hytner (who produced *Miss Saigon*) with great visual richness and new staging.

Rodgers and Hammerstein's third collaboration, *Allegro* (1947), is about a doctor—urged on by his ambitious wife—to make a career in the fashionable world of Chicago. In the end, he recognizes that money does not lead to happiness. He returns to his idyllic town, where human relationships are still intact and he is needed as doctor.

1943 – 1957

Mary Martin in the premiere of *South Pacific* sang "I'm Gonna Wash That Man Right Out of My Hair" while literally washing her hair on stage.

With *South Pacific* (1949), set on a Pacific island during the Second World War, Rodgers and Hammerstein turned to the immediate past. Set against the backdrop of the war against the Japanese, two love stories on the theme of racial prejudice are told: An American nurse renounces her love for a French plantation owner because he has had two children with a native woman. At the same time, a U. S. marine lieutenant and an island girl fall in love. On a dangerous military mission, the lieutenant is killed, while the French plantation owner is missing in action. The nurse swallows her prejudice, goes to care for the brown-skinned children, and then marries her beloved when he finally returns. *South Pacific* was the first musical to show the horror of war and the first hugely popular show to speak out against racism. It was awarded the Pulitzer Prize for drama.

The King and I (1951) is based on the diaries of Anna Harriette Leonowens, who from 1862 to 1867 was the governess to the children of King Mongkut of Siam. The mutual misunderstandings between Western and Eastern culture gave the show a current of tension. The relationship between the English governess and the king, who is interested in Western civilization, but is at the same time a despotic ruler, is depicted as complex: Despite their opposing viewpoints on human rights and the relations between men and women, the patriarchal king and the prim Englishwoman develop mutual sympathy and understanding.

Although Rodgers and Hammerstein's next musicals, *Me and Juliet* (1953), *Pipe Dream* (1955), and *Flower Drum Song* (1958), were all financial successes, none was quite the smash hit of their earlier work. Their final collaboration was *The Sound of Music*, which opened in 1959. In 1960, Oscar Hammerstein died. For *No Strings* (1962), Richard Rodgers wrote his own song lyrics—something he had

never done before. He hired well-known lyricists for his following musicals, but he never settled into a comfortable partnership again,

neither with Hammerstein's protégé Stephen Sondheim, who wrote the lyrics for *West Side Story* and was establishing himself as a composer in his own right, nor with Alan Jay Lerner (who collaborated with Frederick Loewe on *My Fair Lady*), nor with Sheldon Harnick (who wrote the lyrics for *Fiddler on the Roof*). His works in the 1960s and 1970s showed he was, in his later years, losing his connection with the spirit of the times and with public taste, though he worked until his death in 1979 on more musicals, of which only the last, *I Remember Mama*, was not a commercial success.

The Masterworks: Berlin and Porter

Irving Berlin's *Annie Get Your Gun*

Rodgers and Hammerstein worked on Broadway not only as authors but as producers as well. They had hired their idol, Jerome Kern,

Rodgers and Hammerstein with choreographer Jerome Robbins created an amusing and at the same time touching sequence in *The King and I* with "Shall We Dance?" In music and dance, spirited movement and sudden pauses, the unmentioned erotic tension between Anna and the King of Siam is made clear. His performance in *The King and I* made Yul Brynner an international star.

In *No Strings* (1962), a love story without a happy ending between a white journalist and a black fashion model, Richard Rodgers catered to contemporary taste through the renunciation of strings and a realistic narrative. Visible set changes and the position of the musicians on the stage were among the production's innovations.

1943 – 1957

The setting of *The Sound of Music* is Salzburg, Austria, in the 1930s. Maria, a novice nun charged with caring for the seven children of the widowed Baron von Trapp, wins the sympathy of her charges and the love of the baron with her cheerful artfulness and leading family choral singing.

1943 – 1957

to write the music for a musical about the historical sharpshooter Annie Oakley, who toured the West as a member of Buffalo Bill's Wild West exhibition. But Kern died of a stroke in November 1945. The producers then asked Irving Berlin if he wanted to compose the music for the project *Annie Get Your Gun*. Berlin hesitated: He knew there was a difference between his work for revues, or for the recording industry, and stage music that had to be developed according to plot and character. He asked for a week to think it over. When he met with Rodgers and Hammerstein again, his mind was not yet made up, but he had written a few numbers just to test the waters. Among these was "There's No Business Like Show Business." Was this all right?, he asked them. The astounded producers said yes. The music for *Annie Get Your Gun*

Ethel Merman proved her comic talents in the title role of *Annie Get Your Gun*, which offered such ironical pearls of wisdom as "You Can't Get a Man With a Gun" (with the memorable line, "But they don't buy pajamas for pistol-packin' mamas ..."). Merman also surprised the public with her touching dramatic acting.

(1946) is rife with energetic up-tempo numbers like the previously mentioned hymn to the entertainment industry, "There's No Business Like Show Business," clever duets like "Anything You Can Do (I Can Do Better)," and emotionally genuine ballads like "They Say It's Wonderful." Irving Berlin's knack for developing a whole song out of an everyday sentence and a simple musical phrase is particularly evident in "Anything You Can Do": The joking rivalry between the smitten sharpshooter Annie and Frank turns into a comic singing contest, to see who can hold a note longer or sing higher or "sweeter." *Annie Get Your Gun* was the first of a musical subgenre based on biographies of show business personalities. Berlin wrote the music to three more of this type of musical; *Call Me Madam* (1950), the most successful of the three and equally distinguished by Ethel Merman (the original Annie Oakley) in the lead, is a political comedy about a "hostess with the mostes'" who is appointed Ambassador to Lichtenburg by President Truman.

Cole Porter's *Kiss Me, Kate*

Like Irving Berlin with *Annie Get Your Gun*, Cole Porter also had misgivings when the husband-and-wife team of writers Bella and Sam Spewack invited him to write the songs for their adaptation of Shakespeare's *The Taming of the Shrew*. Both Porter's last ventures had been flops. Even his brilliant, melancholy song about the pain of parting, "Every Time We Say Goodbye I Die a Little," had not been able to save the revue *Seven Lively Arts*; and the extravaganza *Around the World in 80 Days*, based on the book by Jules Verne and produced and directed by Orson Welles, closed after only a few performances. After the successes of Rodgers and Hammerstein, Porter was well aware that the days when he could simply write his songs and not worry about the rest were over. But he resisted the temptation to withdraw and enjoy his wealth in peace. The result was *Kiss Me, Kate*.

The show is a play within a play and offers the attractions of a peek backstage—something Shakespeare himself might have contrived: For a musical version of Shakespeare's comedy about the courtship of the man-hating Katharina by the ladies' man and fortune-hunting Petruchio, the "producer" and

Irving Berlin's *Annie Get Your Gun*—seen here in a 1997 production in Germany—is based on the true story of Annie Oakley, who beat her husband, sharpshooter Frank E. Butler, in a shooting contest. Other historic figures who show up in the musical include the famous hunter and circus entrepreneur Buffalo Bill Cody and the legendary Sioux chief Sitting Bull, who starred for a year with the marksman pair in Buffalo Bill's Wild West Exhibition.

1943 – 1957

Kiss Me, Kate: As Petruchio, Fred can put his refractory wife Lilli, who plays Katherina, over his knee with impunity. This is a scene from the 1953 movie, with Kathryn Grayson and Howard Keel.

Kiss Me, Kate: With their literary recommendation to "Brush up Your Shakespeare," the two crooks prove that eight years in the prison library have not been totally wasted on them. Scene photo from the original Broadway production, 1948.

"leading actor" Fred Graham hires his ex-wife Lilli Vanessi for the leading lady. Old feelings and conflicts erupt as soon as the tryouts begin. The romantically involved supporting actors add their own rowdy arguments: Bill accuses Lois of promiscuity, and she responds with "Always True to You in My Fashion" and reproaches him for his gambling in "Why Can't You Behave?" Lilli wants to leave the show because Fred is flirting with Lois. Two gangsters (who bring a kind of wiseguy's innocence to backstage life with "Brush Up Your Shakespeare") are after Fred because Bill has forged his name on a bad check. The conflicts among the cast members merge with those of Shakespeare's scene in Padua, as everyone slugs it out both backstage and onstage. As in Shakespeare, the "shrew" is tamed and the pairs of lovers are reconciled.

Cole Porter's music fills in gaps in the book, and perhaps appropriately so, since no one could introduce language in this setting to rival the poetry of Shakespeare's play: Thus, the Viennese waltz "Wunderbar" expresses the romantic feelings that persist between Fred and Lilli, their radiant memories and their ironic distance from these feelings. Porter uses the contrast

between the modern framing plot and Shakespeare's Italian renaissance world to showcase all conceivable musical styles from high and low culture. Lilli's serious and touching aria "So In Love," in which she admits to herself that she still loves Fred, contrasts with the cool jazz of "It's Too Darn Hot." Madrigals and other Renaissance musi-

cal elements are quoted, while "Brush Up Your Shakespeare" harks back to the popular American Bowery waltzes of the turn of the century. The score is a perfect blend of Porter's unique verbal and musical intelligence and wit.

Cole Porter, like many of his contemporaries, made something of a foray into classic musical theater forms with *Out of This World*, which carried on the tradition of the operetta. Unlike Richard Rodgers or Frederick Loewe, however, he did not look back to the later sentimental works of the form, but followed the trail and his own temperament back to the more impudent and frivolous works of Jacques Offenbach. Like *Orpheus in the Underworld*, *Out of This World* is a mythical farce: The story uses the myth of Amphitryon, whose wife is seduced by the god Zeus in the shape of her husband. In the musical telling, an American couple in modern Greece meets Jupiter descending from Mount Olympus, lusting as usual for an affair with a mortal. Jupiter is accompanied by his eloquent sidekick, the god Mercury, and pursued by his jealous wife, Juno. Never before had Porter composed such a self-contained and ambitious musical, but a ponderous libretto and prudish contemporary tastes forestalled the expected success on Broadway.

Can-Can (1953) illuminated turn-of-the-century Paris with more luck. The proprietress

Porter's *Out Of This World* deals, as Jupiter's first song points out unmistakably, with the pleasure of sex. The Boston magistrate at the 1950 tryout found some costumes too skimpy and some lyrics too suggestive. The producer was issued a list of specific changes to make.

Can-Can gave Cole Porter another opportunity to pay homage to Jacques Offenbach and to Paris. Poster for the 1960 movie starring Shirley MacLaine and Frank Sinatra.

Porter's last stage musical, *Silk Stockings* (1955), was an adaptation of Ernst Lubitsch's elegant film comedy *Ninotchka*. The role of the Soviet commissar Ninotchka, originally played by Greta Garbo, who succumbs in Paris to the charm of the city and capitalism, was taken over on Broadway by Hildegarde Neff. Her leading man was future movie star Don Ameche.

of a dance hall challenges the local authorities by staging a provocative can-can in which she seduces the conscientious district attorney. Porter paints the French local color with

songs like "C'est Magnifique" and "I Love Paris." Near the end of his career in 1956, Porter wrote some of the songs for the movie *High Society*, with Bing Crosby, Grace Kelley, Celeste Holm, Frank Sinatra, and Louis Armstrong as himself. In the years before his death in November 1964, Porter lived in seclusion.

New Names: Loesser and Styne

Frank Loesser's *Guys and Dolls*

While the old hands Irving Berlin and Cole Porter created their masterpieces, some younger composers broke through with works that remain among the most produced of the classic musicals. Frank Loesser's *Guys and Dolls* is one. Loesser, born in 1910 in New York, first made a name for himself writing lyrics for hit songs by Jule Styne and Hoagy Carmichael before he also turned to composing. He celebrated his Broadway debut in 1948 with a much admired musical setting of Brandon Thomas's comedy potboiler *Charley's Aunt*. The critics marvelled at Loesser's musical accomplishment. Two years later, Loesser topped *Where's Charley?* with *Guys and Dolls*. The book of *Guys and Dolls*

Ray Bolger as Charley's aunt in Frank Loesser's *Where's Charley?*

1943 – 1957

Frank Loesser's *Guys and Dolls*

was written by Jo Swerling and Abe Burrows based on short stories by Damon Runyon. Originally the producers were seeking a serious and romantic love story in the style of Rodgers and Hammerstein. Eleven authors tried to fill the bill, but finally Burrows rescued Swerling's earliest attempts by turning the book into a musical comedy. He and Loesser worked with producer George S. Kaufman to create a world of petty crooks, gamblers, and showgirls in the Times Square of the 1920s. The action begins with a bet: The gambler Sky Masterson brags he can seduce any woman in the world, and bets his acquaintance Nathan Detroit that he can take any woman Detroit designates with him to Havana. Nathan points to the Salvation Army missionary Sarah Brown. In the process of winning the bet, however, Sky and Sarah fall in love. Sarah is disheartened when she learns of the bet and rejects Masterson, who she believes only took her with him in order to clear the mission for Nathan Detroit's crap game. Sky, honorably in love, tells Nathan he did not take her to Havana and pays Nathan the $1,000. To save Sarah's mission, which is about to be closed for lack of success at saving sinners, Sky takes on all the players at Nathan's crap game, staking $1,000 per

man if he loses, against each gambler going to a prayer meeting at the mission if he wins. He wins, of course. When Sarah hears that Sky did not collect on his bet against Nathan, she is convinced of his worthiness and the

Guys and Dolls: The Happy Ending. The long-beloved Nathan cures his eternally congested fiancée Adelaide of her psychosomatic symptoms. Scene photo from the 1994 Broadway revival starring Tony-Award winners Nathan Lane and Faith Prince.

Frank Loesser's *The Most Happy Fella* (1956) is a folk piece about Tony, an elderly Italian winegrower in California, who proposes to a young waitress by letter. Since she does not know him, he is afraid she will scorn him because of his age and appearance, so he sends her a photo of the young worker Joe. Rosabella agrees to the wedding but falls in love with Joe, who she discovers is only a hired hand. Out of sympathy for Tony and love for Joe, by whom she is pregnant, she remains on the winery. Rosabella and Tony, who is willing to adopt her child, remain together. Scene photo from the original Broadway production.

How To Succeed in Business Without Really Trying: The brazenly ambitious J. Pierpont Finch becomes popular with his superior singing his university anthem with him. Scene photo from the 1961 New York premiere.

two are married, at a double ceremony with Nathan and his long-time fiancée, Adelaide.

Loesser's eclectic music contrasts jazzy ballads with hymns and rhythmic ensemble numbers with gospel songs and canons. A group of "tinhorns" sing an artful fugue, and in the lament of the frustrated night club dancer Adelaide, blues elements meet psychoanalytic vocabulary. Theater critic Kenneth Tynan reviewed the 1952 London opening of *Guys and Dolls* in his best rendition of Runyonesque/Masterson/Detroit-speak: "Personally, I found myself laughing ha-ha last night more often than a guy in the critical dodge has any right to. And I am ready to up and drop on my knees before Frank Loesser ... In fact, this Loesser is maybe the best light composer in the world." What Loesser apparently knew was that the stylistic diversity of his music may not please every musical ear, but it is a constituent part of great musical theater. Six years after *Guys and Dolls*, Loesser wrote *The Most Happy Fella*. Despite the classically trained voices of the opera stars he hired for the production, and despite an opulent score with over thirty musical numbers joined by recitatives—which vary between typical Broadway ballads, Italian folk motifs, and operatic arias and duets—Loesser insisted that his work was not an opera but an "extended musical play."

With *The Most Happy Fella*, Loesser had seized on Gershwin's idea of "American folk opera." His next show, *How To Succeed in Business Without Really Trying*, on the other hand, was a biting satire on ruthless ambition in the business world. Most musicals revolve around a central love story; but the opporunistic J. Pierpont Finch, who climbs the corporate ladder from window cleaner to chairman of the board, addresses the show's only love song, "I Believe in You," to his own reflection.

Frank Loesser's protégés, composer Richard Adler and lyricist Jerry Ross, set their 1954 comedy *The Pajama Game* in the working world. This show, which deals with the conflicts between union and management of a pajama factory, also featured choreographer Bob Fosse in his debut. The team's next comedy, *Damn Yankees* (1955), is about a baseball fan who sells his soul to the devil to help his "Washington Senators" to beat the all-powerful "New York Yankees." Jerry Ross's death in 1955 damaged the promising career of the composer Richard Adler, who, without his partner, did not repeat his early successes.

Jule Styne

Jule Styne had six long-running Broadway hits among the twelve shows he wrote between 1947 and 1964; yet he is a lesser-known composer compared with names like Berlin, Porter, or Rodgers. Born in 1905 in London, Styne grew up in Chicago from the age of eight. His songs, including "Diamonds Are a Girl's Best Friend" and "People" are more closely associated with their interpreters like Marilyn Monroe or Barbra Streisand than they are with their author. Comediennes like Judy Holliday in *Bells Are Ringing* or Ethel Merman in *Gypsy*, Carol Channing in *Gentlemen Prefer Blondes* or Streisand in *Funny Girl*, owe a measure of their success to Styne, who wrote their signature songs. *Funny Girl* tells the story of revue star Fanny Brice, who sings "I'm the Greatest Star" to

In *Damn Yankees*, an aging baseball fan is led into temptation not only by the devil but also by the witch Lola. Jerry Lewis starred as the devil in the 1996/97 revival.

1943 – 1957

Funny Girl in a 1997 performance in Munich.

97

convince legendary producer Flo Ziegfeld to hire her for his *Follies*, even though Brice did not conform to the beauty ideal of the time. This dynamic and frantic comic aria of self-promotion reflects Styne's sure feel for effective show numbers, which often (including the case of "Diamonds Are a Girl's Best Friend") can be delivered to the audience with a wink.

Styne graduated from piano and composition studies in the 1920s in Chicago, just at a time when his hometown was superseding New Orleans as the center of jazz. Styne's early 1930s jazz ensemble employed legendary soloists, including Benny Goodman. On the way to Hollywood, Styne

Ethel Merman and future television star Jack Klugman in the premiere of *Gypsy*. Merman's powerful character study of the ambitious mother of Gypsy Rose Lee contributed substantially to the success of the show. Like Cole Porter in *Anything Goes* or Irving Berlin in *Annie Get Your Gun*, Jule Styne wrote songs tailor-made for Merman's voice and persona.

took a detour through Broadway; his debut production was the 1947 gangster comedy *High Button Shoes*. *Gentlemen Prefer Blondes* (1949) was based on the short stories of Anita Loos and paid homage to the jazz age and the musical comedies of the 1920s. Jule Styne remained faithful to musical comedy throughout his career. He teamed up with Betty Comden and Adolph Green for *Two in the Aisle* (1951) and the trio went on to write many well-known shows. In 1956 they brought out *Bells Are Ringing*, produced and choreographed by Jerome Robbins, about a shy switchboard operator who falls in love with the voice of a writer. Many of Styne's musicals are set in the entertainment industry: *Say, Darling* (1958) is based on the actual experiences of novelist Richard Bissell on the production of *The Pajama Game* which

1943 – 1957

Bissell wrote with Richard Adler and Jerry Ross; *Fade Out, Fade In* (1964) is set in 1930s Hollywood; *Do Re Mi* (1960) deals with corruption in the music business; and his most famous musicals, *Funny Girl* and *Gypsy*, are in the biography tradition started by Irving Berlin's *Annie Get Your Gun*—the former about Fannie Brice, the latter based on the autobiography of striptease artist Gypsy Rose Lee.

Gypsy (1959) may well be considered Styne's most mature work. The road from the idea of a musical about Gypsy Rose Lee to the finished stage production was a long one. From the beginning, Ethel Merman was the choice to play Rose, the ambitious stage mother who wants her daughters to be vaudeville stars seemingly at any price. Several authors were approached but refused the project; Cole Porter and Irving Berlin both gave the producers the cold shoulder. Jerome Robbins, who was slated to produce and choreograph the show, brought in the young lyricist of West Side Story, Stephen Sondheim, as a possible composer but Ethel Merman declared that she wouldn't take the role unless they hired an experienced composer. It was Merman who insisted on Jule Styne, and thus Styne wrote the music to Sondheim's lyrics.

Lerner and Loewe: *My Fair Lady*

Composer Frederick Loewe and writer/lyricist Alan Jay Lerner set out in the 1950s to compete with Rodgers and Hammerstein with musicals in the operetta tradition. When Lerner and Loewe's *My Fair Lady* opened in New

A 1997 German production of Gypsy.

Gypsy Rose Lee (née Rose Louise Hovick) as "Queen of American Burlesque" elevated the striptease to a glamorous art form, which

she later performed in top night clubs and on television. She also appeared in Broadway productions, including Cole Porter's *Dubarry Was a Lady*. Her sister Ellen performed in Hollywood films under the stage name June Havoc and played a lead in Rodgers and Hart's *Pal Joey*. This musical contains the song "Zip," meant as hommage to Gypsy Rose Lee.

1943 – 1957

Stage photo of the premiere of *My Fair Lady* with Julie Andrews as Eliza Doolittle and Rex Harrison as Henry Higgins. *My Fair Lady* takes place in 1912 Edwardian London. The misogynist linguist Higgins bets with his acquaintance Colonel Pickering that he can make an 18-year-old Cockney flower girl named Eliza Doolittle into a lady of society despite her rough dialect and indelicate expressions, if she will allow him to work on her speech. After weeks of tortuous work, Eliza learns not only to pronounce sentences like "The rain in Spain falls mainly on the plain" properly, but to think and express herself clearly. Higgins and Pickering show her off at an embassy ball, where she becomes the center of attention. After he has won the bet, Higgins still treats Eliza condescendingly. She erupts in anger, reproaches him for his arrogance, and leaves. Only now he observes how very much she matters to him. To his surprise and delight, she does return to him.

York on March 15, 1956, it broke the box office records set by *Oklahoma!* It remains today one of the most performed musicals around the world and many think of it as the quintessential musical. Two of its songs, "I Could Have Danced All Night" and "On the Street Where You Live" made it to the pop charts before the show opened in New York. At the Tony Awards, *My Fair Lady* walked off with nine awards—virtually all the awards given to a musical in any given year—including, of course, Best Musical. Within a few years the show ran in all the major cities of the Western world. Even in Moscow, where *My Fair Lady* was presented as part of a cultural exchange, it was so well received that a Russian version was hastily produced with the title *Mya Prekrasnaja Lady*. The extravagant movie version, with Rex Harrison and Audrey Hepburn (who acted but did not sing the part of Liza Doolittle), won the Academy Award for Best Picture in 1964 and has become a much-loved classic of musical cinema.

My Fair Lady was the brainchild of producer Gabriel Pascal, who fought for years for the rights and realization of this project: Unfortunately, he did not live to see his ideas turned into such triumphant success—he died in 1954. Pascal had first proposed the idea of developing a musical from George Bernard Shaw's play *Pygmalion* to Lerner and Loewe two years earlier. The duo worked for six months on the material and finally gave up—as had Richard Rodgers and Oscar Hammerstein, whom Pascal had also set to work on it. In 1954, Lerner and Loewe took another stab at the material. This time they felt they had successfully adapted *Pygmalion* in a manner that was true to Shaw's dialogue to a previously unheard-of extent.

Shaw's original story refers to an old Greek mythological motif, treated by Ovid in *Metamorphoses*, of a king who falls in love with a statue of an ideal woman (Pygmalion is the name of the king, not the woman). In Ovid, the statue comes to life. Traditionally, Shaw's Eliza has been played on stage mostly by actresses in their thirties and forties, but *My Fair Lady* took Shaw at his word and cast the young Englishwoman Julie Andrews. That the British actor Rex Harrison, playing Higgins, could not sing did not faze the producers. When Lerner and Loewe asked Harrison if he could sing, and the actor candidly replied he could sing about four notes, the authors reportedly asked him, "Which four?" They ingeniously turned Harrison's limited vocal range into a kind of talk-singing that was well suited to Professor Higgins's inability to express feelings. Many of the musical numbers unfold naturally out of the action, as when Eliza's breakthrough in elocution leads her and Higgins and Pickering into a spontaneous celebration in "The Rain in Spain," or when Eliza unleashes her frustration with Higgins in "Just You Wait." The metamorphosis of the Cockney flower girl into the

The 1964 film version of *My Fair Lady*, with Audrey Hepburn in the title role, was the most expensive Hollywood production to date.

My Fair Lady: Eliza's father, the rag dealer Doolittle, calls on his drinking buddies to "get me to the church on time." Scene photo of the premiere with Stanley Holloway as Alfred Doolittle.

self-possessed lady is likewise expressed in Loewe's music.

The influence of Viennese operetta on Frederick Loewe's melodies is unmistakeable. Loewe was born in Vienna in 1904, the son of a German operatic tenor Edmund Loewe.

Brigadoon, by Alan Jay Lerner and Frederick Loewe, was made into a movie in 1954, starring Gene Kelly and Cyd Charisse.

1943 – 1957

He grew up with the works of Johann Strauss and Franz Léhar—his father had played Danilo in *The Merry Widow*. Like Kurt Weill, he studied in Berlin with Ferruccio Busoni, performed at the piano with the Berlin Symphony as a youth, and at the age of fifteen composed the hit "Kathrin, du hast die schönsten Beine von Berlin" (Kathrine, You Have the Most Beautiful Legs in Berlin). In 1924, he came to the United States on tour with his father, but decided to remain there. The path to success was thorny: He worked as a bar pianist and scraped through for years as a riding teacher, professional boxer, mounted mailman, and something of a gold digger. He was still earning a living in bars in 1942 when he approached the young lyricist Alan Jay Lerner about collaborating. Lerner, son of a millionaire, born in 1918, had studied at Harvard and Oxford and written numerous scripts for radio broadcasts. At first there were setbacks for Lerner and Loewe: Even having George Balanchine as producer and choreographer could not make a success out of their first effort, *What's Up*. With *The Day Before Spring* in 1945, the breakthrough came: The show ran 165 performances and a Hollywood studio bought the film rights. With their 1947 musical *Brigadoon*, Lerner and Loewe made their permanent mark on the New York theater world. This show told the magical story of two American tourists who discover the village of Brigadoon in the Scottish highlands, which only emerges from the mists every hundred

The "Fair Lady": Julie Andrews as Queen Guenevere in Lerner and Loewe's *Camelot*.

years. The score was filled with Loewe's Scottish-flavored melodies. The choreography by Agnes de Mille, including a Scottish sword dance, helped paint the exotic milieu. *Brigadoon* was followed four years later by the Western comedy *Paint Your Wagon*, which told of the boom and bust of a Gold Rush town. Loewe's European-style score, including Viennese waltzes, clashes with the quintessentially American setting. This may have contributed to the production's mediocre run on Broadway. It ran four years less than their subsequent masterpiece *My Fair Lady*. In 1958, Frederick Loewe contributed the songs to the film *Gigi*, based on a novel by Colette with a script by Lerner. Set in Belle Epoque Paris, it includes "Thank Heaven for Little Girls" and the spirited "The Night They Invented Champagne." The triumph of *My Fair Lady* raised everyone's expectations for their next stage work: This turned out to be *Camelot* (1960), the story of a love triangle (Arthur/Guinevere/Lancelot) with a mythical setting; it was an extraordinarily expensive production for the time. *Camelot* reunited much of the *My Fair Lady* team—Loewe, Lerner, producer Moss Hart, choreographer Hanya Holm, set designer Oliver Smith, musical director Franz Allers, and leading actress Julie Andrews. Richard Burton as King Arthur was a newcomer to Broadway. Despite lukewarm reviews, which criticized a hackneyed plot and absence of catchy tunes, *Camelot* rode on the coattails of *My Fair Lady* through 873 performances. Frederick Loewe subsequently retired. Not until 1973 could Alan Jay Lerner persuade him to contribute four new songs for the stage version of *Gigi*. Lerner collaborated henceforth with other composers with varying degrees of success.

Finian's Rainbow: Only two months before *Brigadoon* was produced in 1947, another musical on Celtic fairy tale motifs opened on Broadway: *Finian's Rainbow*, with music by Burton Lane. The goblin Og pursues Finian, who has stolen his pot of gold, to

America. There Og transforms a racist politician into a black and himself into a mortal for the love of a woman. Despite a long run and much applause for his songs, Lane only rarely composed stage music. In 1965 he collaborated with Alan Jay Lerner on *On A Clear Day You Can See Forever*. The movie version of *Finian's Rainbow*, with Fred Astaire, was produced in 1968 by Francis Ford Coppola.

1943 – 1957

Leonard Bernstein's *West Side Story*

If *My Fair Lady* was the masterpiece of the operetta-based musical tradition, *West Side Story* with music by Leonard Bernstein and lyrics by Stephen Sondheim, which opened on September 27, 1957, was the apogee of the jazz-oriented stream. All of Rodgers and Hammerstein's achievements in *Oklahoma!*— the integration of story, music, and movement, the dramatic function of songs and dances— reached new heights and plumbed new depths (of meaning, that is) in *West Side Story*.

In 1949, choreographer and producer Jerome Robbins had proposed to Bernstein and author Arthur Laurents a modern musical version of Shakespeare's tragedy *Romeo and Juliet*. The project was originally called "East Side Story" and was going to tell the story of the star-crossed love of a Jewish boy and an Italian-American Catholic girl against the background of violent fighting between rival youth gangs. Other commitments prevented Bernstein and Laurents from immediately taking up the idea. When the time came to begin work in 1957, the authors shifted the setting to the West Side. Inspired by current newspaper stories, they replaced Shakespeare's noble Montague and Capulet families with two street gangs, the established (working-class, second-generation white) Jets and the upstart (newly immigrated Puerto Rican) Sharks. Robbins and Bernstein took six months to cast the production; they assembled a very young ensemble with no stars; the performers could plausibly play teenagers. Tony, a former Jet, and Maria, newly arrived from Puerto Rico and the sister of the Sharks' leader Bernardo, fall in love with each other at first sight at a dance. They defiantly hold fast to their love through the repeatedly flaring conflicts between the hostile

William Shakespeare's *Romeo and Juliet* provided the story for *West Side Story*, with music by Leonard Bernstein. Arthur Laurents' book faithfully follows the dramatic construction of the tragedy and transports the renaissance tragedy without artificial modernism into 20th-century New York. The classic "balcony" (really a window) scene takes place on a fire escape: Carol Lawrence as Maria and Larry Kert as Tony sing "Tonight" in the original production.

gangs. However, when Tony's best friend Riff is stabbed by Bernardo, who is in turn killed in the heat of the moment by Tony, the tragedy takes its relentless course: Just as the separated lovers have been reunited, Tony is killed. The story departs from Shakespeare's ending in what is almost a technicality: where Juliet dies, the despondent Maria survives, but her spirit and innocence are as good as dead.

The spirited dances of the 1961 movie version of *West Side Story* were choreographed by Jerome Robbins.

Even more than Laurents' tight dialogue, Jerome Robbins' breathtaking choreography pushes the action forward. Never before has the story of a musical been told so urgently through dance and music, which led some critics to describe it as a "ballet-opera." Bernstein portrayed the violent conflicts in West Side Story with a piece of music, "The Rumble." Robbins choreographed the dramatic music with stylized theatrical dance as well as naturalistic movements that expressed the explosive sense of menace. There were no "chorus lines" of synchronized choreography; instead, Robbins gave each dancer an individual and characteristic gesture repertoire. Just as Tony and Maria's first encounter and their falling in love at the dance found nonverbal expression in music and movement, so too Tony's death and Maria's pain are conveyed through the language of the music theater. Bernstein struggled long with the idea of writing a large aria for the mourning Maria, but ultimately decided against

1943 – 1957

Choreographer Jerome Robbins (middle) at work on *West Side Story*. Robbins literally worked out each step and every gesture individually with the dancers.

"[The chief problem is] to tread the fine line between opera and Broadway, between realism and poetry, ballet and 'just dancing,' abstract and representational. Avoid being 'messagey.' The line is there, but it's very fine ..."
Leonard Bernstein, *West Side Story* log, March 17, 1956

"There stands that tragic story, with a theme as profound as love versus hate, with all the theatrical risks of death and racial issues and young performers and 'serious' music and complicated balletics—and it all added up for audience and critics."
Leonard Bernstein, August 20, 1957

it. Instead, Tony's death and Maria's grief are expressed in the gradual silencing of their voices during the finale. If song is often an expression of feelings that can no longer be contained, the loss of voice, of the ability to sing here is yet another escalation in emotional pitch. The orchestra alone completes the melody of "Somewhere," as it plays over the silent procession with which the show fades away. Even seemingly simple songs, like "I Feel Pretty," have complex structures. Bernstein also wove a kind of finely spun harmonious net between musical numbers. With Tony's romantic transfiguration "Maria" and the exultant love duet "Tonight," Bernstein and Sondheim wrote popular songs with overwhelming emotional effect, while "Gee, Officer Krupke" confirms a mastery of comic effect as well. In the quintet, he artfully fuses the the Jets' and Sharks' hate-filled fight songs with Maria and Tony's euphoric "Tonight." The orchestration of the entire score shows a jazz influence that is not limited to early jazz elements like blue notes and syncopation, which were already widespread on Broadway. Bernstein brought in more current jazz developments like "cool jazz" and integrated them with classical compositional techniques like twelve-tone rows.

West Side Story's successful balance of the tragic and the comic, of realistic contemporary setting and timeless artistic form, and its fusion of drama, music, dance, and dialogue have remained unmatched in musical theater.

A musical whirlwind

Leonard Bernstein was born in 1918 in Lawrence, Massachusetts, and, like Berlin and Gershwin, was the child of Eastern European Jewish immigrants. By the mid-1950s he had established his reputation as one of the most

Jets and Sharks in *West Side Story*. Scene from the Munich State Theater, Germany, 1997.

scintillating musical talents of the 20th century. He became famous overnight on November 13, 1943 when he stepped in as a last-minute substitute for the ailing conductor Bruno Walter and conducted the New York Philharmonic without rehearsal and in street clothes. Only a few months later, the much-heralded premiere of his *Jeremiah Symphony* took place in Pittsburgh; shortly after that, the ballet "Fancy Free" opened, with music by Bernstein. This piece, choreographed by Jerome Robbins, is about three sailors on shore leave in New York. Robbins proposed that Bernstein take the material of the ballet and turn it into a musical comedy. Without re-peating a single musical phrase from the ballet score, Bernstein composed new songs and again made musical history: On December 28, 1944 his first musical *On the Town* opened on Broadway. The libretto by Betty Comden and Adolph Green leads the three sailors Gabey, Chip, and Ozzie through twenty-four hours in Manhattan against the backdrop of the Second World War. Gabey falls in love with the picture of the current "Miss Subway" Ivy Smith. His two buddies want to help him search for her, but they meet other women, with whom they spend the day. The typical tourist Chip meets the emancipated taxi driver Hildy, the proletarian intellectual Ozzie meets the nymphomaniac Claire. Gabey follows Ivy, but loses sight of her. The three pairs meet up again, after some

On the Town in a 1995 performance at the Academy of the Arts in Berlin.

The jubilant mood after the Allied victory in World War II lives again in this famous V-J Day photo by Alfred Eisenstaedt, which documented the celebrations in Times Square.

1943 – 1957

Candide enjoyed success with its 1974 revival. Leonard Bernstein's musical, like Voltaire's satirical novel, was about a philosopher Pangloss, who always claims to live in the "best of all possible worlds," and the simple Candide, who despite all disasters and blows of fate unshakably holds this conviction.

1943 – 1957

West Side Story: The spirited, Latin-American inspired ensemble number "America."

complications, in the amusement park at Coney Island. As their 24-hour shore leave comes to an end, the three sailors say goodbye to the women and return to their ship. *On the Town* reflects America's optimism in 1944 about the outcome of the war. Bernstein's music carries this exuberant mood and the bantering comedy: His enthusiastic, fresh, and jazzy up-tempo songs, like Hildy's ambiguous "I Can Cook Too," glow in every phrase. Next to ballads like Gabey's joyful "Lucky to Be Me" Bernstein juxtaposed the touching farewell quartet, "Some Other Time," and the effervescent anthem to the city, "New York, New York." Bernstein met *Oklahoma!*'s depiction of an idealized rural America with urbane, jazzy music, complete with a post-Oklahoma obligatory dream ballet.

In the ensuing years, Bernstein moved between the worlds of classical and popular music, courted a youthful public both via television with "The Joy of Music," and also in his famous "Young People's Concerts" with the New York Philharmonic Orchestra, conducted in major concert halls around the world, and composed orchestral works and the one-act opera *Trouble in Tahiti*. In 1953 he found time for his second musical comedy *Wonderful Town*, a further tribute to metropolitan New York, renewed with a libretto by Comden and Green. In this show, two quarreling sisters from the country, the self-confident Ruth and the dreamy Eileen, come to the city where, after some initial difficulties, they find an apartment, jobs, and boyfriends. In 1956, Bernstein wrote *Candide*, with a libretto based on the novel by the French Enlightenment philosopher Voltaire.

For *Candide*, with playwright Lillian Hellman as librettist and poet John Latouche as lyricist, Bernstein assembled a high-power, high-brow

team. He combined masterly waltzes, tangoes, mazurkas, and serenades with jazzy melodies, and created the most extraordinary score heard to date on Broadway. The overwrought book, unfortunately, did not suit the theater-going public, and *Candide* closed after only 73 performances. Only a year later, *West Side Story* opened to mostly favorable reviews and audiences, though few recognized it at the time as a masterpiece. The comparatively meager 732 performances were surpassed by *The Sound of Music*, *My Fair Lady*, and Meredith Willson's *The Music Man*, which also won the Tony Award that year for Best Musical. Until this time, immediate commercial success on Broadway was the definitive criterion for the worth of a show; now, however, an appreciation began to grow in the media and in people's minds for musicals as potentially enduring works of art. Time, ultimately, would tell what was a truly great musical and what was not.

Leonard Bernstein at a rehearsal for *West Side Story*.

1943 – 1957

The Music Man (poster): Meredith Willson's mild satire on American small-town life deals with a kindly impostor who persuades the rural population of Iowa to start up youth orchestras. In this way the self-appointed "Music Professor" brings the enjoyment of music to the Midwest. Willson, a veteran radio performer, was 55 years old when he made his Broadway debut with *The Music Man*. The subject offered the composer and librettist a chance to write spirited marches in the style of John Philip Sousa as well as an occasion to compose folkloric ballads.

1957 – 1978

Separate ways: Musicals and pop culture

Within forty years, the musical soared from a relatively coarse form of entertainment and a wan imitation of European work to an authentic American art form. Leonard Bernstein had blazed new trails. Still, while the form attained new artistic heights with shows like *My Fair Lady* and *West Side Story*, something was changing, and this something was at first barely perceptible, though it would reverberate down to the present.

Since the end of the Second World War, American musical theater and the popular music industry had been closely bound together. All of the most successful composers of popular music sooner or later tried their hands on Broadway. No sooner had jazz spread from New Orleans to Chicago and then throughout the world than the first Blue notes and syncopated rhythms were heard on Broadway. Then, in the mid-1950s rock'n'roll burst on the scene, and in no time at all the charts were topped by names like Elvis Presley, Jerry Lee Lewis, and Little Richard. The American music theater, once seemingly in the vanguard, remained remarkably unaffected. Where once the ambitious, young white composers had eagerly absorbed the jazz sounds created by self-taught black musicians after the war, now Broadway's professional composers scorned the vital but raw rhythms of rock, which somehow did not suit their lofty musical tastes. At the same time, the rock'n'roll generation steered clear of theater music, written mostly by composers on the far side of fifty (at a time when to be over thirty was considered incomprehensible!). As if the supposedly outmoded music of Broadway weren't bad enough, the advent of "muzak" (insipid background music) in department stores, restaurants, and businesses also surely contributed to public distaste. The muzak arrangers frequently took well-known melodies by Kern, Porter, or Berlin and melted them into undifferentiated auditory pulp. No surprise, then, that the emerging musical talents turned to models like Chuck Berry and Buddy Holly. Had things been different, talented song writers like Paul Simon, Brian Wilson, or Paul McCartney might well have found their way to the musical. But now, a generation gap opened: While the younger generation for the most part turned away from the musical and toward rock music, the Broadway audience aged. In 1964, the English Beat bands suddenly conquered the American charts.

And yet, Jerry Herman's title melody from *Hello, Dolly!* won the Grammy for best song of the year, beating out Lennon and McCartney's "A Hard Day's Night." It might take a while for institutions like the Grammy Awards to catch up with the changing times, but the schism between musicals and pop culture was unmistakable.

Charles Strouse in 1960 with *Bye, Bye, Birdie* was the first, and for a long time the only, Broadway composer to use—however ironically—rock'n'roll rhythms. The story, about teen idol Conrad Birdie who must report to the military and with a nationwide television appearance bids farewell to his screeching fans, satirizes the Elvis Presley cult.

At the beginning of the 1960s, the changing of the guard among theater composers had little effect. Leonard Bernstein turned back to devote his energy to his work in classical music. Cole Porter had withdrawn from the theater and then died in 1964. Irving Berlin's last musical, *Mr. President* (1962), dedicated to John F. Kennedy, was a failure. Richard Rodgers found no new lyricist to equal the likes of Lorenz Hart or Oscar Hammerstein. Frederick Loewe gave up composing completely, as did Frank Loesser after *How To Succeed in Business*. Into their shoes stepped a new generation of composers, but only a few, like John Kander or Cy Coleman, would succeed consistently. Some, like Burt Bacharach, made brief forays into Broadway,

1957 – 1978

Promises, Promises (1968) is about an ambitious insurance company employee who curries favor with his superiors by making his apartment available to them for sexual escapades. Burt Bacharach, with his catchy "Popsongs," was one of the few popular composers to find success on Broadway since the 1950s. A musical perfectionist, however, he preferred the studio to the stage. This adaptation of Billy Wilder's touching comedy *The Apartment* remained Bacharach's only musical.

while others, like Meredith Willson or Mitch Leigh, showed early promise but then seemed to stall in their careers. The most accomplished composers of the new generation showed little interest in expanding the genre's horizons. The exception, of course, was Stephen Sondheim.

Diversity and stagnation

While movies, music, fine arts, and the theater sought new and sometimes radical forms and directions, the rebellious mood of the 1960s found no voice on Broadway. Hardly a single musical brought the mood and conflicts of the time to the stage. The popular musical theater seemed content to replay or reinterpret the subjects and styles of previous decades. For the Broadway audience, this meant a series of top-notch productions, all of which harked back to the great performances of the past. Stylish productions, imaginative technology, and well-crafted books masked the textual and musical stagnation. Abstract settings and suggestive lighting effects superseded the previously more naturalistic stage settings. Musical comedies as always were quite popular. Productions like the realistic drama *Golden Boy* or the tantalizing treatment of the rise of the Nazis in *Cabaret* covered the range of musical subjects. A few new musical impulses emerged in the folkloristic milieu of the Yiddish shtetl of Anatevka in *Fiddler on the Roof* or the Spaniard Cervantes in *Man of La Mancha*.

The directors: From staging to directing

More and more often productions were associated with the name of their directors, rather than with their composers or authors. George Abbott, Jerome Robbins, Gower Champion, Bob Fosse, Harold Prince, and Michael Bennett (many of them originally dancers and choreographers) helped even weaker works enjoy long runs and became reliable guarantors (in the minds of the investing "angels") of box-office success. Through the 1950s, the Broadway director's role had been to rehearse the piece with the performers and to bring it adequately to the stage. Now that the musical was regarded as a work of art as a whole, the director gained influence and clout. The concept of integration demanded an artistically responsible personality, someone who was fluent in the different theatrical languages who could give the whole production a uniform style. Directors *cum* producers now actually initiated projects and hired composers to write new songs. Of course, the producer, as the keeper of the purse strings, had the last word on who was on the payroll, but some directors began to produce so that they too could pull the strings.

The 1960s

Intimate theater: *The Fantasticks* On May 3, 1960, off Broadway at the Sullivan Street Playhouse in Greenwich Village, a musical

Producer and choreographer Bob Fosse with Shirley MacLaine at a rehearsal for the filming of *Sweet Charity*.

1957 – 1978

opened with only a handful of characters, five musicians, and an almost empty set. After one week of mixed reviews and moderate audience response, the producer wanted to close the show. Then, however, the show's name spread by word of mouth, and attendance figures grew.

The allegorical chamber play *The Fantasticks* went on to run in the same small theater for over 35 years. The play, based on a comedy *Les Romantiques*, by Edmond Rostand (author of *Cyrano de Bergerac*) has become the single most performed musical in history, with more than 11,000 productions in the United States alone. In Shakespearean fashion (indeed, it is the same story portrayed by the Rustics in *A Midsummer Night's Dream*), a narrator introduces the characters, appeals to the spectators to compensate for the deliberately minimal sets with their imagination, and then slips into another role, to drive the plot forward.

The authors, Harvey Schmidt and Tom Jones, had worked together since their student days at the University of Texas. Jones wrote the lyrics, and Schmidt, who could not read music, wrote the songs, among them ballads of unique melodic charm like "Much More" and "Try to Remember." The producer David Merrick employed the pair on Broadway, where their show *110 in the Shade* opened in 1963. Richard Nash's adaptation of his play *The Rainmaker* tells the love story between the lonely farmer's daughter Lizzie and the "Rainmaker" Bill Starbuck, who is received by the Texan population like a Messiah during a draught. Schmidt and Jones followed this in 1966 with another small-scale musical, *I Do, I Do*, which tells the story of a marriage, beginning with the wedding night and revolving around an aging couple and their four-poster bed. *I Do, I Do* demonstrated Schmidt's skill for intimate and sensible musical structure. Broadway, however, had to do without their talents. After the success of *I Do, I Do*, Schmidt and

The Fantasticks varies the Romeo and Juliet (Pyramus and Thisbe) theme with comic pretence: Two neighbors *want* their two children Luisa and Matt to fall in love and marry. They feign a quarrel and erect a wall between their properties. The fathers then egg the narrator on to feign Luisa's kidnapping. Matt intervenes and so impresses Luisa with the faked rescue that their marriage is predestined. After initial happiness, mistrust creeps in between the lovers as they learn of the intrigue of their fathers. However, after a period of separation and temptations, Luisa and Matt find each other again. The original production of *The Fantasticks* featured Jerry Orbach, who began his major Broadway career with the role of the Narrator.

ones withdrew to work on more experimental music theater forms in their Portfolio Studio. The fruits of this work were only rarely shown in public.

Timeless music: *Hello, Dolly!*

No one was less interested in

experimental theater than Jerry Herman, born in 1932 in New York City. Herman was interested in composing beautiful and catchy melodies; no one dissociated himself as vehemently from current trends of popular music as he did. This traditionalist found his models in the glamorous scores and materials of the past. The realistic, contemporary *Milk and Honey* (1961), however, did not live up to the standards for timeless music in the style of an Irving Berlin or a Frederick Loewe. The story, set in Israel, follows the love of two older American tourists against the background of the emerging Jewish state. But in 1964, with *Hello, Dolly!*, Herman found his style. The title song, as interpreted by Louis Armstrong, was already on the charts before the New York premiere. *Hello, Dolly!* is based on Thornton Wilder's play *The Matchmaker*, which is itself a revised version of Wilder's earlier play, *The Merchant of Yonkers*. *The Merchant of Yonkers*, moreover, refers back to an 1842 play by a Viennese folk theater playwright and comedian, Johann Nepomuk Nestroy. Nestroy in turn borrowed the material from an English farce called *A Day Well Spent*. So *Hello Dolly!* paid homage, in a sense, to the roots of the musical. At the center of the story stands the widowed marriage broker Dolly Levi, who has been asked by the rich merchant Horace Vandergelder for a match with the milliner Irene Molloy. Dolly, who

Cast with celebrities Robert Preston and Mary Martin, the two-person show *I Do, I Do* was not produced in a studio theater but played on one of the large Broadway stages. The performers, aided by Oliver Smith's stage settings, were able to fill the room.

1957 – 1978

Hello, Dolly! was originally conceived as a starring vehicle for Ethel Merman who bowed out, however, saying she no longer wanted to appear in extended runs. Instead the show starred Carol Channing, who had leapt to stardom in Jule Styne's *Gentlemen Prefer Blondes*. During its original run, the lead was played by stars like Ginger Rogers and Betty Grable. To break the record of *My Fair Lady* and to reach a new audience, the producer David Merrick hired a new, all-black ensemble centered on Pearl Bailey and Cab Calloway. Six years after the premiere, however, Ethel Merman finally played the part once planned for her.

Angela Lansbury in 1966 played the title role in Jerry Herman's *Mame* on Broadway.

would like to become Mrs. Vandergelder herself, attains her goal through a series of cleverly woven intrigues and on the way also forges a relationship between Irene and Vandergelder's young employee, Cornelius.

Herman's next success came in 1966 with *Mame*, which was thematically similar to *Dolly*. The comedy about the lusty former show business star Mame, who against her better judgment must raise her orphan nephew in conservative fasion, is set in the 1920s and 1930s. This allowed Herman to compose romantic melodies and dances in the glamorous style of that time. Later failures—*Dear World* (1969, based on *The Madwoman of Chaillot* by French dramatist Jean Giraudoux) and *Mack and Mabel* (1974)—and a plagiarism suit over his melody for *Hello, Dolly!* took their toll on the composer. *Mack and Mabel*, the love story between the film pioneer and inventor of slapstick Mack Sennett and his star Mabel Normand, remains an unknown masterpiece. Many imitators had already copied Jerry Herman when he made a surprising comeback in 1983 with *La Cage aux Folles*. The book, written by Harvey Fierstein, and based on a French film of the same name, centers on gay nightclub owners and longtime domestic partners, George and Albin, and on the starring female impersonator in their

club. A year before, Fierstein had taken Broadway by storm with his multiple-prize-winning play *Torch Song Trilogy* and its unblinking portrayal of homosexuality. In 1985, a retrospective revue of Herman's music was produced on Broadway, called *Jerry's Girls*.

Folklore and drama:
Fiddler on the Roof

Composer Jerry Bock and lyricist Sheldon Harnick made a name for themselves with *Fiorello!*, a sympathetic biography of popular New York Mayor Fiorello La Guardia, and the romantic comedy *She Loves Me*.

Then, in 1964, with librettist Joseph Stein they staged a great coup. *Fiddler on the Roof*, based on stories by the great Yiddish writer Sholom Aleichem, tells the story of the dairyman Tevye and, for those unfamiliar with Yiddish culture, illuminated the unique culture of the East European shtetl (before they were essentially eliminated from the world). Tevye lives with his wife and five daughters in the Ukrainian village Anatevka during the time of the czar. Constantly threatened by antisemitic pogroms, his main worry is to find prosperity and happiness (i. e., in marriage) for his daughters. The daughters, however, resist their father's plans: Tzeitel prefers a poor tailor to the wealthy butcher Tevye has chosen, Hodel loves a revolutionary student whom she follows into exile to Siberia, and Chava horrifies the orthodox Tevye when she marries a gentile Russian. The show ends with the czar expelling the Jews from their home. Tevye and his wife Golde hope for a better future with their two youngest daughters in America. Just as Boris Aronson's sets were inspired by the shtetl paintings of Marc Chagall, Jerry Bock's songs—especially "If I Were a Rich Man" or Hodel's farewell ballad "Far from the Home I Love"—were inspired by hasidic folkways and the particular klezmer music of the shtetl. The mixture of drama and sentiment, folklore and melancholy wit, against all prediction, appealed to a broad public: *Fiddler on the Roof* ran longer than than any other previous theater production on Broadway.

The male "ladies" of the nightclub greet their public. *La Cage Aux Folles*, the successful adaptation of the French film focused on a drag show, though in other respects quite a conventional work, proved Jerry Herman's undiminished talent for catchy melodies and glitzy show numbers. The song "I Am What I Am" became an anthem of sorts for the Gay and Lesbian rights.

Fiorello! (1959), by Jerry Bock and Sheldon Harnick, was the third musical awarded the Pulitzer Prize for best drama of the year.

1957 – 1978

The title *Fiddler on the Roof* comes from a recurring image in the paintings by Marc Chagall: The fiddler on the roof, who tries to eke from his instrument a few pretty sounds without breaking his neck, stands as a symbol for the Jewish communities of Eastern Europe that endured poverty and antisemitism.

1957 – 1978

With their work on *The Rothschilds* (1970), a not completely historically accurate biography of the German Jewish banker Meyer Amschel Rothschild, Bock and Harnick quarreled and their partnership came to an end.

Stark realism: *Golden Boy*

In 1964, Charles Strouse and Lee Adams wrote the music to *Golden Boy*, a dramatic musical about the rise and fall of a boxer. In contrast to Clifford Odets' play by the same name, on which the musical was based, the hero of the musical is a black man, full of ambition to escape the ghetto, and full of anger over the racism he experiences. The fight which could make him a sports hero is his last: His adversary dies from a hard blow and he dies in a car accident. The choreographic representation of the fight, along with the sharp realism of the show's dialogue, is one of the most impressive qualities of the production. The leading actor, Sammy Davis, Jr., was celebrated for his energetic performance as the "Golden Boy."

The impossible dream: *Man of La Mancha*

It started with a newspaper story about a television scriptwriter, Dale Wasserman, who was making inquiries in Spain to prepare for an

A 1993 German production of *Fiddler on the Roof*, which in Germany was produced under the title *Anatevka* (the name of the village in the show).

adaptation of *Don Quixote*, the 17th-century Spanish novel by Miguel de Cervantes. The result of Wasserman's efforts was a television movie. Entranced by the material, Mitch Leigh persuaded Wasserman to produce a musical, rather than the

planned play. Leigh had studied music at Yale with, among others, Paul Hindemith, and made so much money writing advertising jingles that he occasionally wrote theater music gratis. For his score to *Man of La Mancha*, he was inspired by Flamenco, Bolero, and other forms from Spanish

The climax of *Golden Boy* was the boxing match with a fatal ending. Scene photo from the New York production.

folklore. The orchestra, set up in two sections on either side of the stage, not only played to accompany the individual songs but also often underscored the dialogue, thereby creating a fluid transition between drama and song. The success of *Man of La Mancha* in 1965 realized an impossible dream for the composer: The material was considered so out of the mainstream and the creators were so unknown that the show was first produced off Broadway. With "The Impossible Dream," Sancho Panza's candid tribute "I Really Like Him," or the angry and desperate song of Aldonza, Mitch Leigh created powerful and original music, which gave rise to great expectations. Leigh, however, abandoned the musical theater after two subsequent flops.

The film classic *All About Eve*, starring Bette Davis, was adapted into a musical in 1970 called *Applause*. It starred Lauren Bacall as the aging diva and was another success for the team of Strouse and Adams. Charles Strouse, who like Leonard Bernstein had an excellent musical education, had composed symphonic works and chamber music. For Broadway he provided effective stage songs. *Annie* (1977), a sentimental story somewhat reminiscent of Dickens' *Oliver Twist*, about an orphan child who is adopted by a kindly multimillionaire, was his largest box-office success without Lee Adams.

Comedy and jazz: Neil Simon and Cy Coleman

Neil Simon, best known for the long string of comedic plays that ruled Broadway—from *The Odd Couple, Barefoot in the Park, Plaza Suite,*

1957 – 1978

Richard Kiley (left) as Don Quixote in *Man of La Mancha*. A framing device shows the author Cervantes in the dungeons of the Spanish inquisition where he and his servant play out the story of the Knight of the Woeful Countenance for their fellow-prisoners: A confused old man calls himself Don Quixote and imagines the part-time-prostitute Aldonza to be a virtuous princess Dulcinea. In her honor he takes off with his servant Sancho Panza on a series of windmill-tilting forays against imaginary adversaries. Aldonza tries by harsh measures to make him see their true identities, but Quixote insists he must continue to "dream the impossible dream, to fight the unbeatable foe." When at last he recognizes his pitiful reality, he dies. The redeemed Aldonza, however, now carries on his ideals.

1957 – 1978

to *Brighton Beach Memoirs* and *Biloxi Blues* (among others)—was also involved in a short string of musicals. Simon wrote five musical scripts, with his characteristic pointed dialogue and well-oiled comedic dramaturgy. After *Little Me* (1962) came *Sweet Charity* (1966), both with music by Cy Colemen; Burt Bacharach wrote the songs to *Promises, Promises* (1968), an adaptation of Billy Wilder's Academy Award-winning movie *The Apartment*. Simon's two-person show, *They're Playing Our Song* (1979), had music by Marvin Hamlisch and lyrics by Carole Bayer Sager, while Hamlisch also composed the songs for *The Goodbye Girl*, a 1993 musical restaging of an earlier Simon play.

Born in 1929 in New York, former concert pianist and jazz musician Cy Coleman took his time in coming to the theater. When some of his songs, like "Witchcraft" (written for Frank Sinatra), became hits, he was commissioned to compose his first musical. The result was *Wildcat*. He followed this in 1962 with the songs to Neil Simon's zany farce *Little Me*, in which Belle Poitrine, a legendary diva, tells with false modesty of her rise from poverty to fame and wealth, and of the men in her life. These were all embodied by television comedian Sid Caesar, who performed the song "Boom-Boom" as a fantastic parody of Maurice Chevalier. Applauded by the critics, the public reception, despite Coleman's spirited, jazz-inspired music, was disappointing. Simon and Coleman had more luck in 1966 with *Sweet Charity*, the tragicomic story of the candid dance-for-hire girl Charity, who believes despite her disillusioning work and repeated unhappy affairs that she will someday find true love. The show is based on Federico Fellini's film *The Nights of Cabiria*. *Sweet Charity* ran for eleven years, no doubt partly owing to e choreography of Bob Fosse. oleman had another success with *Love My Wife* (1977) about two married couples who attempt to keep pace with the sexual revolution, only for the husbands to discover that they genuinely love their wives.

Sweet Charity in a 1996 performance in Germany. The dynamic ensemble number "There's Gotta Be Something Better than This," harking back to Leonard Bernstein's "America," along with "Big Spender" shows Cy Coleman's jazz heritage.

Snapshots in time: From *Cabaret* to *Chicago*

Where *Golden Boy* had treated contemporary material realistically, the 1966 show *Cabaret* offered a snapshot of Weimar Germany as it descended into Nazism. Based on the autobiographical stories by British author Christopher Sherwood, *Cabaret* ostensibly revolves around a love affair between a young romantic Chris and the "Tingel Tangel" singer Sally Bowles, who appears in the somewhat disreputable Berlin Kit Kat Club. A subplot tells of Fräulein Schneider, the boarding house mistress, who rejects the proposal of the Jewish fruit vendor Schultz because of the impending fascist regime. Sally and Chris's relationship fails when she becomes pregnant and has an abortion. The script by Joe Masteroff departed from the Sherwood material in a few key respects: Sherwood's bisexual Englishman Cliff became a heterosexual American, and Sally becomes an Englishwoman. Director and producer Harold

Prince entrusted composer John Kander and lyricist Fred Ebb with the songs. Kander and Ebb had worked together the previous year, with Liza Minelli, on their Broadway debut, *Flora, the Red Menace*, the story of

Cabaret: Liza Minelli as cabaret performer Sally Bowles in Bob Fosse's 1972 movie, which earned her an Oscar.

1957 – 1978

George Grosz's paintings from pre-Nazi Germany inspired the creation of *Cabaret*. Detail from *Ecce Homo*.

leftist activists in the 1930s. Kander's skill at suiting his musical means to the tone of the piece and the characters made him one of the most versatile theater composers of his generation. Kander studied Kurt Weill's pre-1933 German compositions for songs like "Money, Money," performed in the Kit Kat Club by Sally and the androgynous emcee played by Joel Grey. The frighteningly rousing song of the young Nazis, "Tomorrow Belongs to Me," suggests sentimental German folk and student songs. The original production offered a degree of authenticity by casting Lotte Lenya, Kurt Weill's widow and a veteran of the original German production of *The Threepenny Opera*, as Fräulein Schneider.

In the nostalgic family comedy *The Happy Time* (1967), Kander and Ebb worked with Joseph Stein (who wrote the book of *Fiddler on the Roof*) on a musical version of a Greek film called *Alexis Sorbas*. *Zorba* (1968) followed the trend of folkloric musicals. In 1975, Kander and Ebb returned to the cynicism and shady ambience of *Cabaret* in *Chicago*. Bob Fosse had wanted since the 1950s to adapt a play by Maurine Watkins. Twenty years later he produced one of the most dismal and

In the successful 1983 revival of *Zorba*, Anthony Quinn took over the part of the wise master of the art of living Alexis Sorbas, which he had already played in the movie.

sarcastic pieces in Broadway history. Behind him lay protracted negotiations with the playwright and her mother, marriage and divorce from his designated star Gwen Verdon, two heart attacks, and bypass surgery (all of which he processed into the movie, *All That Jazz*, which offers a wonderful look at the backstage workings—struggles, rehearsals, cattle calls, addictions—of musical theater). The story of *Chicago*, set in the 1920s, revolves around Roxie Hart, who murders her lover, and not only goes free with the help of her long-winded attorney but also attains a modicum of stardom, which Fosse presented in the style of a vaudeville revue. John Kander's music, reminiscent of the Chicago jazz of the 1920s, and Fred Ebb's lyrics set the sarcastic tone in songs like "All That Jazz" and "Razzle-Dazzle." Kander and Ebb had another success with *Woman of the Year* (1981), and their most recent work, *Steel Pier*, about a dance marathon, opened in 1997.

Chicago. A Viennese production.

Rock over Broadway

The age of Aquarius: *Hair*

There was in the 1960s, without doubt, a schism between pop culture, pop music, and rock'n'roll, on the one hand, and the more conventional musicals that dominated Broadway (and Hollywood). Moreover, inside the cocoon of the Broadway theaters, few mainstream musicals reflected the turmoil taking

place out in the streets and on the college campuses of America. Then, on April 29, 1968, *Hair*, the "American Tribal Love-Rock Musical," opened at the Biltmore Theatre. *Hair* broke a lot of tacit Broadway rules: The music was neither jazz-based nor in the operetta tradition, it was pure, psychedelic rock, amplified, electric, driving. Its characters were neither historical, mythological, fantastical, nor noble; they were young adults, kids, hippies, runaways, draft

Chita Rivera in the London production of Kander and Ebb's *Kiss of the Spider-woman*. The dramatic chamber play of 1992 is set in a Latin American prison. A revolutionary is confronted through his cellmate, a gay shopwindow decorator, with another world view and life-style. A figment of the lively imagination of the shop-window decorator is the "Spiderwoman" Aurora Molina, the memory of a film idol of his childhood. The story of a slowly developing, tragically ending friendship is based on the play and novel of the same name by Manuel Puig.

1957 – 1978

dodgers, marijuana smokers. Songs about smoking pot and dropping LSD, about sex, free love, the Vietnam War, racism, and nuclear fallout evoked a spectrum of passions in audiences, from outrage to cultish enthusiasm. The show originally opened off Broadway, as a production at Joseph Papp's New York Shakespeare Festival; Papp's Greenwich Village-based Public Theater was one of the only thriving venues for more experimental theater in New York. Two unemployed actors named Gerome Ragni and James Rado had written a loose collection of scenes around the draftee Claude (played by Rado), about to be sent to Vietnam. He spends the last days and hours before his conscription among a group of hippies surrounding the charismatic spokesman Berger (played by Ragni). (The show, we should note, was produced long before the cult murders instigated by another charsimatic "hippie" leader, Charles Manson.) Galt MacDermot, the son of a Canadian diplomat with a more traditional musical background, set

Although *Hair* is in many respects an outmoded musical expression of a particular time, its sentiments, Galt MacDermot's simple, charming ballads like "Frank Mills" and "Easy to Be Hard," and rousing up-tempo songs like "I Got Life" or the title song have an amazing freshness. Scene photo from a 1997 production in Lübeck, Germany.

Ragni and Rado's lyrics to music. An enthusiastic financial backer of the original bought the rights and produced the piece in a discotheque called Cheetah; for the move to Broadway six months later, experimental theater producer Tom O'Horgan was brought in. O'Horgan completely restyled Hair, reduced the rudimentary plot to a minimum and asked the authors to write new songs; some of the new songs produced to order were "Sodomy" (whose lyrics are a littany of what were then considered "deviant" sexual practices) or "Hashish" (another littany, this time of illicit and licit drugs from cocaine to shoe polish). O'Horgan took pains to shock the middle class and had the ensemble strip naked (albeit under a gauzy

screen amid a smokey atmosphere)
at the end of the first act. He also
invited audience participation in the
finale, "Let the Sunshine In." With
such well-calculated provocation,
he led a sincere protest against the
Establishment to commercial success, and brought audiences to
Broadway who otherwise might never have
crossed a musical theater threshold. In short, for
a time, O'Horgan bridged the chasm between
commercial theater and rock'n'roll.

The sketches and songs in *Oh, Calcutta!* (1969), to the horror of some critics, treated openly themes like masturbation or fetishism and presented the joyfully shocked public with a nude ensemble.

At about the same time as *Hair*, the so-called
sexual revolution came to Broadway in full force.
For the infamous *Oh, Calcutta!*, English drama
critic Kenneth Tynan invited authors as varied as
Samuel Beckett, John Lennon, and Sam Shepard
to contribute sketches. Many of the production
partners were drawn from the experimental New
York theater scene. The erotic entertainment
revue, with songs by Robert Dennis, Peter
Schickele, and Stanley Walden, attained the
third longest run in Broadway history to date,
and became something of a tourist attraction.

Rock operas

Hair brought rock music to the musical, launching yet another stylistic stream that extends up to
Jonathan Larson's *Rent* (1996). The initially
rudimentary and simple rock'n'roll expanded
into more complex forms in the 1960s. In 1967,
the Beatles' album, *Sergeant Pepper's Lonely
Hearts Club Band*, which took over a month of
studio work, inaugurated a trend away from
simple songs to sound worlds nearly unreproduc-
ible in live performance and to the "concept
album." In 1969, the rock group The Who, led
by Pete Townsend, published their "rock opera"
Tommy, which was reworked and staged as a
full-blown theater production 25 years later.

Tommy, by The Who, is the story of a blind and deaf-mute boy, who turns out in postwar England to be a gifted pinball player and is cured ultimately in a wonderful way. The 1996 show drew some interest, mainly among Who fans, but not a lot.

1957 – 1978

Stephen Schwartz's *Godspell* (1971) was presented Off Broadway production as clown theater.

Stephen Schwartz had composed *Pippin* in his Pittsburgh student days, though it was not produced until after the success of *Godspell* in 1972. The show tells the story of Pippin, the naive son of Charlemagne, who searches in vain, as a warrior, lover, and fighter for social justice, for the meaning of life. The retreat into bourgeois married life finally makes Pippin happy. Bob Fosse, as producer and choreographer of the rock spectacle, and inspired by commedia dell'arte and medieval minstrels, helped the production to a long run on Broadway.

Hair composer Galt MacDermot made a considerable success with his rock songs to Shakespeare's comedy *Two Gentlemen of Verona* in 1971; for the song "Who Is Silvia?" he reached back to the original Shakespeare verses, as he had, in fact, done in *Hair*, when he set Hamlet's speech "What a piece of work is a man" to a simple, plaintive melody. MacDermot was not the only musical theater composer to pirate the great English playwright. In 1968, the same year that *Hair* rocked the stage, Hal Hester and Danny Apolinar also drew their inspiration from Shakespeare for their music to the Off-Broadway production *Your Own Thing*. With electric guitar and a multimedia show, their comedy *What You Want* is still playing in the East Village in New York City. In 1971, two rock musicals opened in New York about the last seven days in the life of Jesus Christ. One of these was *Godspell*, with music by a young composer named Stephen Schwartz. The author and producer John Michael Tebelak intended it as a positive retelling of the events around Christ's crucifixion and resurrection, hoping to appeal to a young audience. To Schwartz's gospel-rock music, ten actors in changing roles narrated and enacted the gospel of the New Testament. The actor playing Jesus was dressed like a circus clown with a Superman emblem on his chest. With such consciously simple and comedic means, *Godspell* achieved a considerably longer run than did

esus Christ Superstar, the pop opera produced by Tom O'Horgan and written by two relative newcomers, Englishmen Andrew Lloyd Webber and Tim Rice.

Cult musicals

In the wake of the early rock operas, a series of shows were produced that lovingly quoted the clichés and myths of Hollywood B movies, or—like Grease—satirized (however mildly) the rock 'n' roll era. With only minimal musical ambitions, some original and refreshing works achieved cult status and captured a younger audience for the musical theater.

The cheerful rock'n'roll show Grease is one of the most-performed musicals of the 1990s. Scene photo from a London production.

The first production of Grease, staged in a Chicago streetcar station, lasted five hours. A pair of producers secured the stage rights, hired Jim Jacobs and Warren Casey for the music,

book, and lyrics, asked them to make necessary cuts, and produced the show in New York in 1972. Riding the crest of a wave of nostalgia, Grease was a terrific success on Broadway.

A 1996/97 German production of The Rocky Horror Picture Show.

The love story between Sandy and Danny supposedly evokes sentimental and enthusiastic memories of high school in the 1950s, of James Dean, greasers, hot rods, angora sweaters, hair cream, and rock'n'roll. It was made into a movie in 1978, with John Travolta (fresh from his fame in Saturday Night Fever) and Olivia Newton-John (fresh off the middle-of-the-road pop charts). The movie spread the fame of this musical around the world, and it is still often produced.

Written and set to music by Richard O'Brien, the Rocky Horror Picture Show likewise attained worldwide cult status when turned into a movie

1957 – 1978

The poster for the original New York production of Alan Menken and Howard Ashman's *Little Shop of Horrors*.

Beauty and the Beast, a stage version of the full-length animated movie produced by Walt Disney Studios, in a 1995 performance at the Viennese Raimund Theater. Alan Menken composed the music, Tim Rice and Howard Ashman wrote the libretto.

in 1975. Made up and dressed in costumes like the bizarre figures of the rock-scored musical, loyal theater and movie fans accompanied the show with their own action and commentaries. The parody on cheap Hollywood productions was first mounted in 1973 in a London playhouse with only 60 seats. The *Rocky Horror Picture Show* varies cleverly with motifs from science fiction and horror films. The story line is basic: A naive young couple in love are stranded and take refuge in a remote castle full of bizarre inhabitants. The transsexual Transylvanian transvestite Frank'n'furter seduces both Brad and Janet, creates an artificial person Rocky as a pleasure object, and feeds his guests the Rocker Eddie, whom he has killed. Ultimately he is done in by his hunchbacked servant Riff-Raff.

Little Shop of Horrors, with music by Alan Menken and lyrics by Howard Ashman, opened Off Broadway in 1982. It is based on a 1960 B movie of the same name by Roger Corman (featuring a very young Jack Nicholson as a masochistic dental patient whose pleasure foils the thrill of the sadistic Dr. Scrivello, D.D.S.). The musical follows the love of the shy Seymour for the salesgirl Audrey, who is involved with a sadistic dentist. Seymour's other love is the carnivorous plant he has raised, Audrey II, whose ever-increasing appetite for blood demands several sacrifices. Alan Menken's music is clearly, and openly, indebted to the songs of the girl groups of the early 1960s—the "chorus" in *Little Shop* is a trio of girls named "Crystal," "Chiffon," and "Ronette"—all of them groups from that period. *Little Shop of Horrors* was also made into a movie, directed by "Muppetteer" Frank Oz, and starring a number of actors who have made their names in television comedy and movies—Rick Moranis, Steve Martin—as well as the original theatrical Audrey, Ellen Greene. Menken and Ashman, unlike many other authors of limited cult shows, went on to tremendous success. Until Ashman's death from AIDS, they wrote the songs, and won Academy Awards, for a string of Disney animated features, including *The Little Mermaid* and *Beauty and the Beast* (which later transferred to Broadway). Menken has since worked with other lyricists, including Tim Rice.

Dan Goggin's enduring Off-Broadway comedy *Nunsense* (1985) is about five nuns who are the only members of their order to escape a deadly case of food poisoning. To raise the considerable burial costs for their sisters, the survivors organize a benefit gala, at which all five reveal their performing talents. Goggins capitalized on the success of his absurd and blackly humorous work with two sequels.

Chicago ranks among the few great works of the 1970s. As the weak husband of the murderess Roxie Hart, Barney Martin sings "Mister Cellophane." A revival of this John Kander/Fred Ebb musical played on Broadway in 1997.

With the pessimistic society comedy *Company* (1970), composer Stephen Sondheim began a series of works, extraordinary in both form and content.

1957 – 1978

The 1970s

Crisis on Broadway

Despite its own success, *Hair* started no revolution. Just as 1968's mood of awakening yielded to disillusionment, the hopes for a general renewal in the American musical theater were also dampened. In fact: In the early 1970s, Broadway experienced its greatest crisis up to that time, for the lack of emerging talent now became painfully apparent. Although *Hair* was imitated, known rock composers stayed away from the musical as a medium. From the generation of the 1960s' composers, only Kander and Ebb and Cy Coleman seemed to produce hits. Harvey Schmidt, Mitch Leigh, and Jerry Bock had withdrawn, and Jerry Herman's projects failed with critics and at the box office. Rising production costs hampered the producer's job of raising the required funding. In lieu of the many private financiers of earlier years, larger corporations stepped in as

Michael Bennett, the creator of *A Chorus Line*, at a real audition for Burt Bacharach's *Promises, Promises*.

"angels"—primarily the major movie companies. Despite the crisis, two very different composers emerged, and both have since then made their mark on the musical: Andrew Lloyd Webber and Stephen Sondheim. Aside from the growing predominance of Sondheim and Webber, the highlights of this decade were Kander and Ebb's *Chicago*, and *A Chorus Line*, conceived by Michael Bennett with music by Marvin Hamlisch.

A look backstage: *A Chorus Line*

On January 18, 1974, at around midnight, 24 company dancers, known as "gypsies," met in a New York dance studio at the invitation of dancer/choreographer Michael Bennett to talk about their calling—its experiences, hopes, and frustrations. He came away from these sessions commenting that "what those kids had been doing was auditioning their lives for me." From the edited tape recordings he made, Bennett worked with writers James Kirkwood and Nicholas Dante to develop the material for a musical. The decline in Broadway musicals of the early 1970s and his indignation over the bad job market for stage dancers prompted Bennett to

1957 – 1978

aim the spotlight on the cadre of anonymous ensemble players. Instead of having the book and music written in the conventional way, by developing the final version through a series of out-of-town tryouts, *A Chorus Line* emerged in two phases. Again, Joseph Papp and the New York Shakespeare Festival were involved. New scenes were written, worked on, expanded, changed, or rejected by the performers themselves. Along came the film composer Marvin Hamlisch and the lyricist Ed Kleban, who set the personal stories in musical numbers. The Oscar-winning Hamlisch accepted the job against his agent's advice and despite the modest salary—the same as for all the other partners—of 100 dollars per week. A first four-and-a-half hour performance was structurally tightened up and shortened by two hours. Three months after the opening in April 1975, *A Chorus Line* moved to Broadway, where it ran until 1990. On the one hand a tribute to the countless ensemble dancers, who work as small cogs in the theatrical machinery, on the other hand an unsentimental look at the ruthless audition system on Broadway, *A Chorus Line* won many awards, including the Pulitzer Prize. The "plot" is framed within a group audition for a musical revue: The choreographer Zach not only tests the dancing abilities of the eighteen remaining applicants, but allows them to speak about personal things, whether they are happy to get a job where they will be only part of a faceless ensemble. As in the midnight discussion session that began the life of *A Chorus Line*, personalities, fates, dreams, and fears were revealed. Paul, a gay man, tells of his pride and his shame over his first job in a

A Chorus Line ends with its only ensemble number, "One," which is a rehearsal for the play within the play.

A Chorus Line: The applicants for a few desirable jobs try to position themselves in the best possible light.

1957 – 1978

drag show; the Puerto Rican Diana reports in "Nothing" of her problems in acting class. Val amuses her rivals in "Dance 10, Looks 3" (better known under the title "Tits & Ass") by singing the praises of silicone and claiming that in auditions looks are at least as important as dancing ability. Another applicant is Cassie, a former lover of producer Zach. He considers her a solo dancer and thus too good for the chorus, but Cassie, facing unemployment, is not ashamed to be part of the chorus. With her emotional appeal, "Music in the Mirror" ("Let Me Dance for You") she entices the reserved Zach out of his shell. Insiders claim to recognize in Zach a self-portrait of Michael Bennett.

Harald Juhnke and Gaby Gasser in a German production of *They're Playing Our Song.*

Autobiographical musicals

The 1970s saw a whole series of musicals based on autobiographies. For example, Marvin Hamlisch and lyricist Carole Bayer Sager treated their own stormy love and work relationship in the songs to Neil Simon's urbane musical comedy, *They're Playing Our Song* (1979). Apart from three background singers, who portray different facets of the protagonists, the show got along with only two characters.

I'm Getting My Act Together and Taking It on the Road (1978), written by Gretchen Cryer with music by Nancy Ford, also showed unmistakable traces of autobiography. Nearing 40, the singer Heather presents her friends and manager with a very personal solo program, which is an expression of her independence as a woman and performer. Her refusal to tailor her act for more commercial success leads to her breakup with Joe. Heather will continue her career even without his support.

Andrew Lloyd Webber
and Stephen Sondheim

Webber and Rice: Biblical themes

In 1970, a record titled *Jesus Christ Superstar* was released. The composer was a mere 21-

year-old Englishman; the lyricist was only slightly older. Respectively, they were Andrew Lloyd Webber and Tim Rice. The former would achieve an

degree of success and acclaim in musical theater scarcely predictable at the time of that record's release. Webber and Rice belonged to a generation that had grown up with rock music. Webber was born in London, March 22, 1948, the son of a church musician and professor of composition and music theory. A magazine for music teachers published his first compositions in 1959, when he was just 11. On the one hand listening to Bill Haley and the Everly Brothers, on the other hand familiar with Prokofiev and Puccini, Webber also enthusiastically attended performances of musicals in London's West End. Tim Rice, by contrast, born November 13, 1944, was not all that interested in musicals; his interest was pop music. Having tried his hand as a singer and composer, he switched to writing song lyrics. In the following years, a pair of little-noticed recordings with songs of Webber and Rice were issued, as well as the never-produced musical *The Likes of Us* about a 19th-century English social reformer. The initially unspectacular commission from a school choirmaster to write a short piece of music on a religious topic for the school festival turned out to have far-

The Bible provided the framework for Andrew Lloyd Webber's first musical. For *Joseph and the Amazing Technicolor Dreamcoat*, Webber turned to the first book of Moses, in which Joseph reports that his eleven brothers—jealous of the colorful coat given to him by their father—sell him into slavery in Egypt. There he rises, thanks to his clairvoyant abilities, to be advisor to the Pharaoh. Illustration from the Koberger Bible of 1483.

A German production, with staging based on the 1982 Broadway production, of *Joseph and the Amazing Technicolor Dreamcoat*.

1957 – 1978

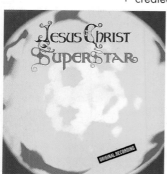

Jesus Christ Superstar: From concept album ...

reaching consequences. Webber and Rice created a 15-minute oratorio that included rock elements, country and western sounds, and calypso rhythms. Presented on March 1, 1968, the work was applauded by pupils and parents. It would have fallen into obscurity, however, had not Andrew Lloyd Webber's father organized another performance two months later in the church where he worked. The father of a choir member who happened to be music critic for the *Sunday Times* also happened to be in attendance and spontaneously wrote an enthusiastic review, which led to more performances. Constantly growing with the addition of new material, the short oratorio developed into the full-length musical *Joseph and the Amazing Technicolor Dreamcoat*. The full-length work was first performed in 1976.

From recording studio to stage

Religious themes and spiritual questions were in fashion around 1970: Open-minded church leaders tried to reach the younger generation with gospel and rock music. The dean of St. Paul's Cathedral in London suggested to Webber and Rice that they write a piece based on the New Testament. In late 1969, they released a single with the title "Jesus Christ Superstar." To forestall accusations of blasphemy, the dean himself wrote a foreword that was printed on the record's cover. Somehow a rumor started that then-Beatle John Lennon would appear in the cathedral as Jesus; the rumors were vehemently denied, though, as rumors tend to do, they persisted and delayed the planned performance. In 1966, Lennon had upset Christians around the world by his off-the-cuff remark that the Beatles were more popular than Jesus. In any case, the single did not get very far on the charts. The project *Jesus Christ Superstar* hung by a thread, when strong record sales were reported from the Netherlands and Brazil. The double album then produced sold very well, especially in the United States. Tim Rice's eloquent lyrics have an unaffected, prosaic directness, and, despite Webber's rock instrumentation, the designation "rock opera" is only partially correct: the score is a colorful stylistic melange of show songs, folk ballads, contemporary classical music, Gregorian chants, and rock, revealing above all Webber's intimate knowledge of classical music. Tom O'Horgan was hired to develop a Broadway theater work out of the studio concept album *Jesus Christ Superstar*. The production, which opened October 12, 1971, confirmed O'Horgan's reputation as a provocateur. The critics reproached the producer, who had been contractually guaranteed exclusive artistic control, for a hash of effects and tastelessness. His brash and opulent direction, with homoerotic overtones, met with more than aesthetic objections. Christian groups protested that their religious sensibilities has been offended while the American Jewish Committee claimed that the production and Rice's libretto had antisemitic undertones. Nonetheless, although some critics had hardly a good word for Webber's music and Rice's libretto, the production was in the black barely two years into its run. Many shows have run longer and still never reaped profits.

From *Jesus Christ Superstar* to *Evita*

Jesus Christ Superstar made millionaires of Webber and Rice. They had difficulty, however,

... to Broadway production. Tom O'Horgan's controversial New York production, with spectacular scenery and expensive machinery. Webber was reportedly not happy with O'Horgan's interpretation; the conflict escalated to the point where the producer barred the composer from attending rehearsals. The London premiere in August 1972 was more in line with Webber's ideas and ran eight years in the West End.

1957 – 1978

For a long time, *Jesus Christ Superstar* was Andrew Lloyd Webber's only musical to be made into a movie—until Alan Parker's screen version of *Evita* (1997). An animated adaptation of *Cats* is also planned.

Twenty years after their mutual failure with *Jeeves*, Ayckbourne and Webber produced the show under the title *By Jeeves* in the Scarborough theater, newly purchased by the authors. Instead of opulent scenery and overwhelming special effects, Ayckbourne and Webber relied on the masterly use of simple theatrical means: A car is made twice from two chests and a sofa, a five-piece band plays Webber's sentimental songs in the style of the good old days, while the charming but not very clever dandy Bertie Wooster and his butler Jeeves, the perfect embodiment of British understatement, nonchalantly play their game.

agreeing on what would be their next project: Webber wanted to do a stage adaptation of P. G. Wodehouse's very British stories about the unshakable butler Jeeves, while Rice was taken instead with the biography of the Argentinian First Lady, Eva Perón. Webber therefore collaborated with British playwright Alan Ayckbourne, the author of boulevard comedies. Together, they wrote *Jeeves* (1975), which was Webber's first musical written directly for the theater, his first with spoken dialogue, and for a long time his only failure. Webber's biographer Michael Walsh explains that the musical comedy *Jeeves* was as long as Wagner's ponderous opera *Tristan and Isolde*, but only half as amusing. The show ran for two weeks. Meanwhile, Tim Rice had written the libretto to *Evita*, which, like *Jesus Christ Superstar*, had no spoken dialogue. Webber returned to his long-time partner and to their proven method, first producing a studio recording and then thinking about a theatrical production. The studio album,

boasted Julie Covington as Eva and Colm Wilkinson (who would later gain worldwide fame in *Les Miserables*) as Che Guevara. With *Evita*, in 1978, Webber not only began an extraordinary series of successes, but also the worldwide marketing of grand-scale musicals which eventually ended Broadway's longstanding hegemony.

Stephen Sondheim

If Andrew Lloyd Webber is the most financially successful musical composer of all time, Stephen Sondheim is the most innovative. Working nearly alone and risking financial disaster over and over again, Sondheim has consistently forged new dimensions in the musical in terms of both content and music. Born into a wealthy family, Sondheim studied music at Williams College in western Massachusetts and was backed on his first steps into show music by Oscar Hammerstein. After working as lyricist on *West Side Story* with Leonard Bernstein, and with Jule Styne on *Gypsy*, Sondheim got a chance in 1962 from producer Harold Prince to prove himself as a composer. With the writers Burt Shevelove and Larry Gelbart, Sondheim created a costume farce based on the comedies of the Roman poet Plautus. The result was *A Funny Thing Happened on the Way to the Forum*, about a clever slave Pseudolus, who attains his freedom against all odds through his skillful wrangling and scheming to unite his dreamy, not well-off master with his beloved. In *Forum*, Sondheim draws a direct line from Plautus's ancient Roman comedies to 20th-century American burlesque. To draw in the public for the turbulent farce, Sondheim composed during tryouts the opening number "Comedy Tonight," choreographed by Jerome Robbins, which became the best-known song from the show. Sondheim's next show was *Anyone Can Whistle*, in 1964; it was a depressing setback, but the composer claimed he could accept a flop so long as it attempted something new; he seemed to withdraw from the theater, but in six years he came back.

Musicals for adults

Company (1970) was the prelude to a trilogy of society comedies produced in close collabora-

Stephen Sondheim before the curtain of *Sunday in the Park with George*.

The clever slave Pseudolus in a 1997 German performance of *A Funny Thing Happened on the Way to the Forum*.

1957 – 1978

Company: Between two birthday parties for the thirtysomething Bobby stretches a loosely connected sequence of scenes evincing a pessimistic view of marriage.

Harold Prince was inspired to create *Follies* by a photo of former silent film star Gloria Swanson in the ruins of an old Broadway theater.

Follies rode the crest of a nostalgia wave, which helped, among other things, Vincent Youmans' *No, No, Nanette* to new fame, as something other than a love-filled conjuring of the past.

tion with Harold Prince. With this show, the composer/director team departed from the conventional dramaturgy of the musical comedy: *Company* took as its foundation a series of one-act plays written by the actor George Furth. Working with Sondheim and Prince, Furth expanded four of the one-acts into the musical. Dispensing with an ongoing continuous narrative, *Company* shows snapshots from the life of the upper middle class in Manhattan, similar to Woody Allen's film portraits of urban neurotics. The bachelor Bobby skeptically observes five couples whose relationships make him leery of entering a committed relationship. He sees alienation, alcoholism, infidelity, and hopeless rituals for the preservation of eternal youth with an irony that conceals fear and unreadiness for marriage. Behind the comic facade, the elegance of Sondheim's texts and his virtuosic settings in rhythmically adventurous music—songs such as "The Little Things You Do Together" and "The Ladies Who Lunch"— shine through a sobering view on marriage.

The themes of aging and memory, already suggested in *Company*, are at the heart of *Follies*, another Sondheim-Prince collaboration that opened a year later. Unlike *Company*, *Follies* was an extravagant production and, although it won awards and enjoyed a moderately noteworthy run, it was a financial failure. This did not diminish artistic appreciation of the show. *Follies* is a fictional account of a meeting of former female revue stars with the Flo Ziegfeld-type producer Dimitri Weisman. Sondheim and Prince molded this basis into a distinguished study of transitoriness and the relationship of theatrical illusion with life's reality. The aging showgirls were confronted with their youthful likenesses, with their hopes and plans, and with what they have actually become.

Sondheim's music is seductive; he used reminiscences of the great revues to pay homage to Irving Berlin and Cole Porter, and with his Gershwin satire "Losing My Mind," wrote a song of (for him) unaccustomed feeling.

Sondheim and Prince closed their trilogy of society comedies in 1973 with an adaptation of the Ingmar Bergman's 1955 film *Smiles of a Summer Night*. In *A Little Night Music*, Sondheim wrote an entire musical in three-quarter time. His waltzes, polonaises, minuets, and barcaroles do not allow monotony, and express the historical European ambience of the material without lapsing into nostalgia. The ballad "Send in the Clowns" has become Sondheim's most famous composition. After the ruthless demonstration of lost illusions in *Follies*, *A Little Night Music* took a kinder view of society. *New York Times* critic Clive Barnes praised Sondheim and Prince's work as a musical for adults.

Five lieder singers introduce, like an antique chorus, the plot and characters of Sondheim's *A Little Night Music* in lieu of an overture. The show is set in Sweden at the turn of the century: The no longer young actress Désirée Armfeldt encounters a former lover, attorney Frederick Egerman. Both feel drawn to one another again, but Désirée's affair with a married officer and Armfeldt's marriage to an 18-year-old stand in the way. Frederick's son is in love with his stepmother, who is the same age as he is, while the officer's wife tries to seduce Egerman. Désirée's grey mother is successful in matching up the appropriate couples in the course of a dinner party. While the lovers find each other, she dies unseen and content after a life fulfilled.

Penny Dreadfuls, Paintings, and Grimm Fairy Tales

While 1976's *Pacific Overtures*, despite its unorthodox themes and music, did not find a following with the public, 1979's *Sweeney Todd* was more successful (though it too was not a financial success). The story unfolds like a melodrama or a penny dreadful (inexpensive hack stories that are a Victorian equivalent of pulp fiction); it is based on a sensational bloodthirsty 19th-century drama, itself based on

1957 – 1978

Pacific Overtures tells from the Japanese viewpoint the 1853 opening forced by American gunboat politics to previously prohibited western influences and trade interests. Almost exclusively cast with Asian performers, the production's structure was based on traditional Japanese Kabuki theater, which meant, among other things, that men played the roles of women.

Sweeney Todd in a 1996 German performance.

Merrily We Roll Along tells of three friends who dream of a Broadway career together as composer, lyricist, and author, and of the disillusionment and betrayal of their dream when the composer sells out to Hollywood. Sondheim and author George Furth told the story backwards, beginning the action in 1980 and ending in 1954.

popular myth and indeed on stories told in penny dreadfuls: An exiled (but innocent) barber seeks revenge against the judge who sent him away in order to seduce the barber's wife; in pursuit of his plan, he takes up with a frazzled pieshop proprietor, who suggests that they cook Sweeney's victims in meat pies—"Business needs a lift … think of it as thrift," she coaxes him. Sondheim furnished the grotesque shocker with his first through-composed score and Harold Prince's staging drew a parallel between Todd's homicidal rampage ("the history of the world, my sweet, … is who gets eaten and who gets to eat") and the dehumanization wrought by the industrial revolution.

The commercial fiasco *Merrily We Roll Along* (1982) marked the end of Sondheim's long-time collaboration with Harold Prince. For his next two projects Sondheim worked with author and producer James Lapine. *Sunday in the Park with George* (1984) describes the creative process of works of art against the backdrop of personal and creative crises and the artist caught between his personal vision and the demands of the market. Some critics decried the intellectual narcissism of the ambitious, Pulitzer Prize-winning work. *Into the Woods* (1987) illuminates the mythological and psychological contents of Grimms' fairy tales. Produced in the materialistic and self-seeking 1980s, the show re-

presented a plea for more social responsibility. Different fairy tale motifs are interwoven: To

overcome an evil witch's curse of childlessness, a baker and his wife must find Cinderella's shoe, Little Red Riding Hood's cape, Jack's milk cow, and a strand of Rapunzel's hair. In this they are successful, and everything appears to be going well. But the luck in this world does not last: Death and alienation of some characters spur the survivors to value the common good over their own interests.

Georges Seurat's pointillist painting, *Sunday Afternoon on the Island of La Grande Jatte*, inspired Sondheim's musical *Sunday in the Park with George*.

In *Assassins* (1991), Sondheim assembles a series of historical figures including John Wilkes Booth, Lee Harvey Oswald, and John Hinckley, all of whom either assassinated or tried to assassinate a president. The revue-like series of pictures

suggests the dark side of the American dream. Sondheim again reveals his emotional reserve and cynicism about blame; his music is an intellectual pleasure, but otherwise technical and cold. With *Passion*

Rapunzel lets down her golden hair in the Broadway production of *Into the Woods*.

1957 – 1978

(1994), his latest work to date, he challenged himself to deal with the force of passion without irony: The officer Giorgio stands between two women—his sensual, married lover Clara and the unattractive and sickly Fosca whose obsessive, apparently hopeless love for him overshadows and destroys his relationship with Clara. Although Fosca knows that in her condition it can mean her death,

she sleeps with the love-vanquished Giorgio; three days later, she dies. This adaptation of a film by Ettore Scola again reveals Sondheim's interest in and his intimacy with European culture. His music and James Lapine's book push

Sondheim furnished the grim political parable *Assassins* with cheerful show songs, spirited marches, and a bitter antinationalist anthem. Scene photo of the German premiere.

the action of the one-act play forward in an uninterrupted flow, fusing different narratives and scenes. The correspondence between Giorgio and Clara leads the two, writer and receiver, through a musical dialogue, while the simultaneously played scene from reality shows Giorgio in conversation with Fosca: This scenic and musical montage technique offers an exciting, realistic pictorial and musical version of the ongoing narrative.

Sondheim's standing as the most important currently active musical composer is uncontested. As a lyricist, he stands on a level with Cole Porter and Lorenz Hart, with his lyrics and characterization continually reflected in refined and grammatically adroit rhymes. Sondheim's competence as a composer, who numbers Ravel, Prokofiev, Copland, and Britten among his models, is unquestionable. His orchestral accompaniments, arranged by Jonathan Tunick, are free of the current fashion of locking onto the song melody, and develop a fascinating independent existence. Sondheim compensates for a lack of catchy tunes with compositional finesse: Through insistently recurring motifs, he joins completely different themes in an encapsulated whole and creates atmospheric density. Except for some film music, Sondheim writes almost exclusively for the stage. He has greatly expanded the palette of subjects for musical theater and thus helped fuse the boundaries between entertainment and "serious" music.

For the two-person show, *Marry Me a Little* (1980), two neighboring singles in New York sing Sondheim songs. Photo from a 1997 German performance.

Passion: The officer Giorgio between the two women, Fosca and Clara. Scene photo of the Broadway production.

Singer, actress, dancer, and charismatic stage personality: Liza Minelli in *The Act*, by John Kander and Fred Ebb.

"There're no people like show people" (Irving Berlin, from *Annie Get Your Gun*). What is it that makes an Ethel Merman so great? Or a Liza Minelli? Or a Zero Mostel? Or a Patti Lupone? The musical theater actor is the most versatile of performers. The training is rigorous, and looks don't carry you. Not only do you have to be an expressive singer, dancer, and actor, but you have to remain convincing in the musical's transitions, you have to stay in character, you need stamina, and you need something else—something not quite definable: *presence*.

Because the sweep of the musical production is often on a grander scale, with a song or a dance number functioning as an expression of heightened, or inexpressible, emotion, the singing and dancing actor must be a master of rhythm and timing, and must be comfortable working with an orchestra and choreography, even when they may conflict with his or her internal creative process. When playing an emotionally loaded scene, the musical performer must be alert to musical cues, changes in lighting, nuances, other actors' lines and business, and choreographed dance numbers. While precisely following such carefully planned directions, the musical performer must offer an emotional and personal interpretation of the role, while maintaining technical control.

The human being is at the center of the stage. The great British theatrical and film director producer Peter Brook once explained: "I can take any empty space and call it a bare stage. A man walks across this empty space whilst someone else is watching him, and this is all that is needed for an act of theatre to be engaged." Still, throughout theatrical history, efforts have been made to banish the human actor and his or her insufficiencies from the stage. Gordon Craig, a famous English director and stage designer (and son of the world-famous English, and very human, actress Ellen Terry) in the early part of the 20th century, imagined a theater with no actors, with a kind of puppet to replace humans. This may not be as far-fetched as it sounds (despite the fact that Craig was seeking a new kind of acting): In modern musical productions characters sometimes nearly disappear behind sensational special effects and extravagant lighting and sets. Indeed, where performers like Ethel Merman once had to project their voices, in tune

The Musical Theater Performer 🎭

and in character, to the last row of the balcony, performers themselves now have sound amplification to help them. Presence, then, becomes something neatly packaged. Andrew Lloyd Webber's musicals *Cats* and *Starlight Express* did just fine without stars—and some might argue the real "stars" in these productions are the designers, not the actors, and not the book or score—though each made extreme physical demands on its cast members. Still, after these particular shows, Webber turned from cats and railroads back to subjects centered on real people.

Very few stars—like Liza Minelli or Ethel Merman—actually have pieces written especially for them. Often, the performer stands on a lower level of the totem pole. He or she generally has little or no influence on content or concept, though as the musical is more and more an experiential, unified work of art, that performer is a critical contributor to the final artistic product. Now, when large-scale productions are more or less mass-produced around the world, it may seem impossible for an

Fame takes place in New York's High School of Performing Arts (now La Guardia High School), where students are trained as dancers, musicians, artists, or actors. Rehearsal photo.

individual to leave a mark on a role. Instead, performers will be cast in a role for their very lack of distinction—because they are as much like the original performer as possible.

The demands on the musical performer's voice and body are tremendous. Knowing that even the greatest American stars had individual strengths and weaknesses might reassure the musical's new generation: when Fred Astaire, then exclusively a Broadway performer, was being considered for a studio contract in Hollywood, the studio assessed him as a moderate actor who "can't sing," whose balding head was too large for his slight frame. The note ends, however, with the laconic remark: "can dance." That Fred Astaire became one of the greatest musical performers of all times shows how important personality and presence are in this profession.

Class in musical theater at the Berlin University of the Arts.

Musicals for the world market

In 1982 three musicals written by Andrew Lloyd Webber were playing simultaneously on Broadway and in London's West End. Nothing like that had happened since the time of Rodgers and Hammerstein. This time, however, the author of the dominant musicals was not an American, but a European. What was certainly a personal triumph for Webber was also due to a period of development in which the English producer Cameron Mackintosh played a decisive role.

What we think of as American musicals had always been the outgrowth of commercial interests. American producers considered a run on Broadway the only measure of success and rarely set their sights much further than that section of Manhattan. European entrepreneurs, on the other hand, would have been happy to pay good money for the rights to New York successes, if only they were for sale.

It was Cameron Mackintosh who had the idea to market his successful London productions worldwide, which he produced either personally or through licensed agents and brought to the stage in absolutely identically designed and orchestrated productions. Diverging artistic interpretations of the works were not only unwanted but prohibited by copyright law. Just as cities around the world vie to host the Olympic Games, many European cities vied to become the site of long runs of large-scale productions; to be competitive, they often had to develop their infrastructure by planning appropriate theater venues. The result could be a significant economic boost for communities and regions. The city of Bochum, in North Rhine-Westphalia, Germany, built a theater for 24 million marks with a national subsidy; this theater has been rented since 1988 by the manager of the German-language version of Webber's *Starlight Express*.

The British have shown the Americans a thing or two about marketing and merchandising since the 1980s. There was a time when Broadway productions basically could not remain afloat in the face of unfavorable reviews from the New York drama critics. But with aggressive advertising strategies, advance release of the shows' music, and reputations as box office successes in London, Webber's works proved nearly immune to negative reviews.

Evita marked the beginning of a new era in musical theater. Unlike the standard book musical, the new style was more of a European music drama with a continuous score, with little to no dialogue. Productions like *Starlight Express* and *Miss Saigon*—the latter by the French team of Schoenberg and Boublil—brought back a kind of subgenre that was popular at the end of the 19th century: the extravaganza—powerful spectacles that rely on expensive machinery and mind-boggling special effects. The aesthetics of these performances are reminiscent of opulent cinematic melodramas—as it happens, many of these large-scale productions are based on films and great operas.

Following the musicals of Andrew Lloyd Webber, Cameron Mackintosh also produced works by the Frenchmen Schoenberg and Boublil around the world. Poster for *Les Misérables*.

A critical lesson was learned from the experience with *Jesus Christ Superstar*, which came out first as a record album and only later as a show. Since the 1950s, record sales for original cast albums had often earned more than was ever taken in at the box office, and Andrew Lloyd Webber managed to use the marketing mechanisms of the recording industry, including the "top of the pops" predecessors to MTV on British television, to great advantage. Both "Don't Cry for Me, Argentina" and "High Flying

1978 – today

147

The most successful living theatrical producer, Cameron Mackintosh (b. 1947), began his career as a stagehand. By 1969 he had started to work as a producer. He did not dwell on early failures. Among his more than 300 productions, Webber's *Cats* and *The Phantom of the Opera* as well as Schoenberg and Boublil's *Miss Saigon* and *Les Misérables* have been the most successful.

Adored" from *Evita* were hit singles before the show was ever staged. And although there was no studio recording of Webber's next real smash hit, *Cats*, many of the songs—including the show's most famous number, "Memory"—were made popular with the British public via radio and television so that by the time *Cats* opened in the West End, audiences were already familiar with the music. The London cast recording preceded the show to America. Thus, the show was already making money before it was produced on Broadway, and the entire marketing and publicity machine was ready to make the most of these fruitful beginnings. While Andrew Lloyd Webber produced, or sold, his music within the pop music market as well as within the musical theater world, producer Cameron Mackintosh was able to corner—and in some sense, create—the global market for musicals, including a fair chunk of Broadway. New York music journalists in the late 1980s wrote of a new "British invasion," and *Newsweek* critic Jack Kroll declared that "The English musical sets the tone for international theater."

British musicals

Andrew Lloyd Webber is, of course, not the first English composer to be produced on the American stage. Since Gilbert and Sullivan, there has always been a lively exchange between Broadway and the West End, no doubt facilitated by the lack of the language barriers (Henry Higgins' complaints to the contrary notwithstanding). While there is something unique about the American musical theater—the result of a link of artistic, social, and economic forces—the United States has never been the sole preserve of musical entertainment. In many respects, British theater has had its own musical tradition, with many parallels between London and

New York. The English influence of ballad operas like *The Beggar's Opera* or the operettas of Gilbert and Sullivan on developments in the United States, though extremely strong, is not the only way in which English theater contributed to the musical tradition. For one thing, the commercial American theater system followed an English model that could be considered to reach back to the Renaissance. The British music hall tradition, still alive in some areas and in the traditional English "panto," is not unlike vaudeville, and what Broadway is to New York, the West End is to London: Home of the theaters, and mecca of the tourists. While Braodway has its Tony Awards, London has its "Larrys," named for Lord Laurence Olivier.

English actor, producer, author, renowned dandy, and entertainer Noel Coward also occasionally worked as a composer. The author of witty sophisticated comedies and bon mots was, like Oscar Wilde, a master of self-parody; his acerbic song lyrics make him a British counterpart to Cole Porter. His 1929 operetta *Bitter Sweet*, which as its title promised gave the public a bittersweet love story, was Coward's biggest success on both sides of the Atlantic.

A 1985 production of Noel Gay's *Me and My Girl* was a successful revival of a typical British musical, circa 1937. For the more recent production, the composer's son laboriously reconstructed his father's work, relying on a fragmented stage script and a radio recording preserved on wax disks by the BBC. With some new lyrics by humorist Stephen Fry, *Me and My Girl* leapt to spectacular success and competed with Webber's *Starlight Express* and Schoenberg's *Les Misérables* on Broadway. The society comedy follows the ascent of the cockney Bill

Me and My Girl enjoyed a successful revival in New York and London.

Snibson (played in London and New York by Robert Lindsay), whose noble origin is discovered by chance. He strives ambitiously to copy the social practices of his new class, without losing his own direct and sincere nature. Despite the efforts of his new relatives to help him succeed in proper society, Bill stays true to his friends from his working-class neighborhood, especially one—his own Pygmalion/Eliza Doolittle—who has been transformed into a fine lady. The popular dance, the Lambeth Walk, brings the two classes together.

From the West End to Broadway

In the 1950s and early 1960s, a wave of British musicals flowed from the West End to Broadway. Sandy Wilson wrote the music, book, and lyrics for *The Boy Friend* (1954), with which he parodied the style and subjects of the musical comedies of the 1920s. The story revolved around the wealthy Polly, sent off to a boarding school on the French Riviera. Polly meets Tony, a messenger boy, who conveniently turns out to be the son of a British nobleman. The show was a gentle parody of the earlier style of comedy, with a consistency of voice between its book and its songs. It also was the launching pad for Julie Andrews, whose portrayal of Polly brought her enough acclaim to land the part of the original Eliza Doolittle. Wilson wrote a sequel to *The Boy Friend* in 1962, *Divorce Me, Darling!*, which met with little success.

Wilson's *The Boy Friend* was filmed by Ken Russell starring former fashion model Twiggy.

In 1962 the allegorical musical *Stop the World, I Want to Get Off* by Anthony Newley and Leslie Bricusse successfully crossed the "pond." Narrated by an ancient-style chorus, the show follows the life of a lower middle-class everyman, Littlechap, by means of cabaret and clown theaters. Driven by his ambition, Littlechap rises to be a business bigshot and parliamentarian who ultimately, of course, must come to terms with his inner emptiness. With a production budget of a meager 2,000 pounds, *Stop the World* was also a tremendous hit in New York.

Amid the influx of British musicals around 1960 came the French musical *Irma la Douce*—the first successful transfer from a European capital other than London. *Irma la Douce* came to New York from Paris in 1956, with a book by Alexandre Breffort and music by Marguerite Monnot, after a successful run in London. This same route—Paris to London to New York—would be followed thirty years later by Schoenberg and Boublil's *Les Misérables*. And, just as *Les Misérables* was nursed along by an English Shakespearean director, Trevor Nunn (who directed *Cats* on a hiatus from his classical work), *Irma la Douce* was produced by one of Nunn's most illustrious predecessors at the Royal Shakespeare Company, Peter Brook, who saw the French show and mounted a production in the West End. It is no surprise that neither Brook nor Nunn hesitated to cross over from classical repertory to musical theater. Both had recognized the inherent theatrical potential of music, and had used it impressively in their so-called serious work. For example, Brook handled music brilliantly in a highly nontraditional musical, *Marat/Sade* (by the German playwright Peter Weiss), while Nunn had staged a production of *The Comedy of Errors*—a straightforward Shakespearean production—as a musical comedy at the Aldwych Theater in London in the late 1970s. Both directors, in essence, had the vision to see the musical as a unique form of expression, beyond the

Irma La Douce is about a prostitute with heart, who falls in love with the destitute student Nestor. Out of jealousy, Nestor disguises himself as an English Lord to drive away her other customers. His exhausting double life is complicated by his need to earn the money from which he pays Irma and on which they both live. When he decides to get rid of the nonexistent Lord, he is accused of murder and banished to Devil's Island. His longing for Irma and the news that she is pregnant with his child drives him to escape to Paris, where everything clears up and turns out fine.

Oliver! begins in an orphanage when the small Oliver Twist asks the stingy caretakers for more food: "Food, Glorious Food." Scene photo from a Broadway revival.

1978 – today

Oliver! Oliver meets the picturesque fence Fagin, who engages him, like other boys of his age, as a pickpocket (scene from the 1968 film). Oliver is caught in his first attempt at thievery, but his intended victim, the rich Mr. Brownlow, takes him in because Oliver reminds him of his missing nephew. Fagin and the unscrupulous crook Bill Sikes fear the boy will betray their hideout and have him kidnapped by Bill's mistress, Nancy. Tormented by guilt, Nancy wants to give the child back to Mr. Brownlow; she is killed by the vicious Sikes. He is also killed after a wild chase through the slums of the East End. Oliver proves in fact to be the missing grandnephew of Mr. Brownlow.

boundaries of Broadway or commercial success, and thus helped erase an almost ideological division between "serious" and "entertaining" theater.

Lionel Bart

Lionel Bart's *Oliver!* (1960) gave the British musical its greatest success in a long time. His cockney musical *Fings Ain't Wot They Used T'Be*, which told the story of a once mighty London gang boss, had already demonstrated his extraordinary talent. With the stylish adaptation of Charles Dickens' novel, *Oliver Twist*, Bart was extremely successful. He wrote the book and the song lyrics as well as the music. His imaginative music shows traces of Old English folk songs, hymns, chorales, and dances. The ballad "As Long as He Needs Me," in which Nancy confesses her dependence on the brutal crook Bill Sikes, is one of Bart's most popular works. The great narrative breadth and the many-layered musical form of *Oliver!* suggest Bart as a precursor of Schoenberg and Boublil. His next work was similarly opulent: *Blitz!* bears the stamp of Bart's childhood memories of the German air raids on London during the Second World War. Both this story, about the Jewish family Blitztein, and Bart's subsequent music drama *Maggie May*, set in Liverpool, are quite extraordinary. In the center of the realistic portrayal of this northern English city's docks stands the hardened prostitute Maggie and her young love Casey, who dies trying to stop a weapons shipment to a South American junta. *Maggie May* expressed a social consciousness not often

1978 – today

In the West End, *Blood Brothers* at first seemed unable to hold its own against the competition with more spectacular materials, but the show attained cult status and still stirs a predominantly young audience to tears. Program cover.

voiced in the musicals of the 1960s. Musically, Bart borrows from northern English folk songs, Irish ballads, Liverpool Beat sounds, and shanties.

Blood Brothers

Blood Brothers (1983) by Willy Russell, better known as the author of the comedies *Educating Rita* and *Stags and Hens*, enjoyed one of the longest runs in the West End. Like Bart, Russell, a former hairdresser, is self-educated and like Bart's *Maggie May*, his works bear the stamp of working-class life in Liverpool. *Blood Brothers* is a musical tragedy about an un-employed single mother, Mrs. Johnstone, pregnant again—this time with twins—who takes up the wealthy Mrs. Lyons' suggestion to turn one of the babies over to her. The pact between the mothers assumes that the separated twins will never see each other. Despite belong-ing to different classes, the twins meet when they are eight years old and, unaware of their bio-logical relationship, become "blood brothers." During their childhood they play with their com-mon friend Linda, but then puberty strikes: Both fall in love in Linda, who chooses the working-class Mickey. While Eddie attends university, Mickey loses his job in the factory and goes astray. Broken by a spell in prison, he imagines that Linda cheats on him with Eddie. Mickey's suspicion leads to a deadly confrontation be-tween the two brothers. The story is advanced by a narrator in the style of a ballad singer. The touching and humorous portrayal of the sorrows and small delights of Mrs. Johnstone's family, the innocent and rough child's play, the first love and pressures on the boys growing up border on so-cial kitsch and sentimentality. Still, despite a clear social agenda, *Blood Brothers* is never didactic.

Blood Brothers—here in a German performance in Frankfurt.

1978 – today

153

Commissioned for a Liverpool youth theater, the show was originally conceived as a play, but Russell, an ardent Beatles fan, decided to write a musical and to compose the music himself.

Evita: The model for success

In 1978, with *Evita*, Webber and Rice created the model for the successful European musicals of the 1980s and 1990s. They conceived of a show based on the rise to fame and early death

Evita, played by Patti LuPone in the original New York production. The poor girl who would later become First Lady of Argentina escapes her squalid home at the age of 15 and follows the Tango singer Magaldi to the enticing metropolis of Buenos Aires. There she ascends through affairs with ever more influential men to be a radio moderator, film performer, and ultimately the lover of the officer Perón, who seizes power as a member of a junta. Evita prods Perón to marry her, to strive for autocracy, and to appear as the people's champion. She continues to gain more power herself and wins the affection of the people. Ill with incurable cancer, she gives a final emotional speech and dies at the age of 33.

of the Argentinian First Lady Eva Perón as a continuous-score pop opera. After the single "Don't Cry for Me, Argentina" topped the charts in the fall of 1976, the studio version of the operetta, a double album, was released and met with comparable success. At this point, Webber and Rice approached Broadway producer Harold Prince, who had demonstrated his sensitivity for political and historical subjects with *Cabaret*. Since Prince had other commitments (among them, the original Broadway production of Sondheim's *Sweeney Todd*), *Evita* did not open in the West End until June 21, 1978. It opened in New York just over a year later, in September 1979.

Evita is less a loyal biography than a meditation about the eroticism and fascination of power. Like Orson Welles's classic film *Citizen Kane*, *Evita* actually begins with the announcement of the main character's death, and like *Citizen Kane*, it deals with a posthumous effort, doomed to fail, to unearth the real person behind the icon. Tim Rice's libretto describes Evita's charismatic personality in all her contradictory facets: As a small, poor girl, as a glamorous and radiant beauty, as an avaricious and glacial politician, as a popular and socially dedicated national mother-figure, as a saint and as a whore. Her

pathos-riddled speeches are not completely mendacious, but the expression of a subtle, clever way of thought. With ahistorical sleight of hand, Rice conjures the Cuban revolutionary Che Guevara (who was in reality active a decade later) to narrate the story, offer his commentary, and even to interact and debate with Eva. On the personality cult surrounding Eva, Che comments: "Oh, what a circus, oh, what a show!" However, even with his scorn for the Perón administration, he cannot conceal a certain admiration for "the greatest social climber since Cinderella." Rice's elegant and cynical lyrics set the tone followed by Webber's music, wavering between Latin American rhythms and Argentinian tango. The show met with mixed reviews among the London theater critics. Most gave positive reviews, but

Madonna in Alan Parker's film of *Evita*, which was finally released after a long tug-of-war in 1996. Besides Madonna, names like Barbra Streisand, Liza Minelli, Elaine Paige (the original West End Evita), Bette Midler, Meryl Streep, and Diane Keaton were mentioned for the title character. The film reunited Andrew Lloyd Webber and Tim Rice, who received an Oscar in 1997 for their new song "You Must Love Me."

some reproached the authors for what they saw as the glorification of Evita (a somewhat artistically narrow, literal view)—what would be next, *Adolf Hitler Superstar*? Some strained to see a connection between the subject of this show and their previous success, *Jesus Christ Superstar*, beyond the fact that both title charac-

Tim Rice's libretto for *Chess* was set to music by Benny Andersson and Björn Ulvaeus, the male members the Swedish pop group ABBA. The plot involves a chess duel between an American and a Russian. Inspired by the world championship in 1972 between Bobby Fischer and Boris Spasski, after the proven formula of a continuous-score musical, the show was preceded by the hit song "One Night in Bangkok."

1978 – today

The felines of the Hamburg production of *Cats* have purred continuously since 1986.

ters died at the age of 33 (no credible explanation was proffered, or necessary). The New York press were less concerned with the politics and more dismissive of the music and libretto. But the criticism did not stop the audience from filling the house, and in a surprising about-face, the New York Critics Circle gave *Evita* the award for best musical of the season in 1979–80.

The Return of the Extravaganza

Webber's international successes
Evita has thus far not been followed by another musical from the team of Webber and Rice. In 1986 they composed an eleven-song cycle titled *Cricket* for the birthday of Prince Edward. While Tim Rice may have sought to renew his collaboration with Webber with this project, Webber used melodies from *Cricket* in his own *Aspects of Love* (1989). Rice returned to a longstanding interest he had in writing a musical about Richard the Lionhearted; this turned out to be *Blondel* (1983), with music by Stephen Oliver. Then, using his old tried-and-true formula, Rice wrote the musical *Chess* and produced a studio recording with members of the pop group ABBA, Benny Andersson and Björn Ulvaeus.

Webber's next lyricist turned out to be the late poet

Original drawings for *Cats*:
Top: Grizabella the Glamour Cat
Middle: The Rum Tum Tugger
Bottom: And the legendary Old Deuteronomy.

1978 – today

T.S. Eliot. *Cats* is Webber's settings for a series of poems originally published as *Old Possum's Book of Practical Cats*, which Eliot had written for his godchild. *Old Possum* was a popular children's book in England, and Webber, like Eliot a cat lover, only later thought of fashioning a full-length musical out of the songs. For *Cats*, Webber in 1981 first joined forces with the West End producer Cameron Mackintosh, the artistic director of the Royal Shakespeare Company, Trevor Nunn, and designer John Napier. The show as conceived by the team relied heavily on dance, and Nunn brought in choreographer Gillian Lynne, with whom he has worked at the RSC. There is no dialogue in the show, and the story is a thinly imagined underlying theme, underscored musically through recurrent motifs and snatches of certain songs, rather than anything that might be called a plot. The set is a nocturnal garbage dump, spilling over the stage, on which the "Jellicle cats dance at the Jellicle ball." Nunn and Webber together came up with a frame for the essentially unconnected mini-plays of each of Eliot's poems. The "story" surrounds the question, "When Old Deuteronomy just before dawn, in a silence you feel you can cut with a knife, announces the cat who will now be reborn, and go on to a different Jellicle life ... Who will it be? Who will it be?" The candidates for resurrection then parade across the stage: Rhe domestic Gumbie Cat, the rock'n'roll cat Rum Tum Tugger, the magical Mr. Mistoffolees, or the old theater cat Gus. Finally, after Old Deuteronomy has been abducted by Macavity, "a mystery cat ... [who is] a master criminal that can defy the law," he selects the once-glamorous Grizabella the Glamour Cat, who wallows in memories of better times.

The most popular song of *Cats*, "Memory," is sung by Grizabella. It happens to be the only song in the show not based on a poem by T.S.

Starlight Express presents the dream of a small boy, in which the technically obsolete Rusty races against the ostentatious Diesel Greaseball and the modern E-Lok Electra and prevails. Despite its simple story, *Starlight Express* owes its realization to ultramodern stage technology.

1978 – today

The hydraulically steered, nine-ton heavy steel bridge of the German production of *Starlight Express*.

The Phantom of the Opera (1986) is set in 1861 and tells the story of a mysterious disguised figure who lives in the catacombs of the Parisian opera. To aid the singer he loves, Christine Daaé, and make the performance of the opera "Don Juan" a triumph, the phantom allows a gigantic chandelier to crash on the stage. He kidnaps Christine, who is the only one to see his distorted face. In a grand finale, she successfuly escapes the malefactor and exposes his plan to ruin the opera. Dutch production scene photo.

Eliot. During rehearsals, the producer asked Webber to compose another song and with no more "Practical Cats" to choose from, Webber asked Tim Rice to write a song text. At the same time, Trevor Nunn wrote some verses and preferred them to Rice's work. Nunn's choice netted him a considerable sum in royalties. *Cats* has been the most financially lucrative musical ever, even in the face of its unprecedented (though not unsurpassed) expense. Since its London premiere on May 11, 1981, it has run nonstop in the West End; on Broadway, it opened in 1982 and as of June 1997 broke the previous record for longest run, set by *A Chorus Line*.

Instead of stars, *Cats* relies on Webber's music, Eliot's poetry, and Nunn and Napier's theatrical magic. The finale of the New York production, in which Grizabella and Old Deuteronomy ascend to cat heaven in an enormous tire illuminated by 4,000 lightbulbs, was actually only a taste of things to come—in Webber's next show. First performed in 1984 in London, *Starlight Express*

takes us back to the era of the extravaganza: In the center of John Napier's stage picture stands a steel railway bridge from which roller-skate tracks lead crisscross through the audience and up to the flies. Theaters in London and New York had to be extensively renovated at tremendous expense; but when the prospect of productions in other cities around the world arose, the expense was even greater: In 1988, the German city of Bochum spent 24 million Marks on a theater specifically for *Starlight Express*. The production itself cost another 12 million Marks. Trevor Nunn, in an interview with the

Wall Street Journal, explained that the show rests on the same unspoken premise as Disneyland: "Here is my money, now give me an experience."

When Webber was researching the old Paris Opera for his next undertaking, *The Phantom of the Opera,* he was delighted to discover that, in 1849, in his opera *Le Prophète,* Giacomo Meyerbeer had propelled singers on roller skates and staged special effects like volcanic eruptions with genuine fire. The Paris Opera House was an immense edifice, with underground passages running more than half a mile and an artificial lake in its catacombs. This is the setting of Gaston Leroux's 1911 gothic novel *The Phantom of the Opera,* which inspired many a movie. Webber and Cameron Mackintosh were considering a musical theater adaptation of Leroux's book; in 1976 Ken Hill had borrowed classic

opera and operetta arias from Offenbach, Gounod, Verdi, Bizet, and Mozart in a West End production, but Webber preferred to compose his own. Until *Phantom,* Webber had only composed one work originally for the stage—that was *Jeeves,* and it was a flop. All his other works were originally conceived as oratorios, concept albums, or song cycles. But by now Webber's experience with musical theater had prepared him well for a departure of this sort. Webber wanted to engage Alan Jay Lerner to write the libretto for *The Phantom of the Opera,* but Lerner died in 1986 of cancer. So Webber wrote the book with Richard Stilgoe, with whom he had already collaborated on *Cats* and *Starlight Express.* Like *Evita,* the new show was directed by Harold Prince. *Phantom* offers its share of special effects,

Andrew Lloyd Webber (b. 1948) wrote the role of the singer Christine Daaé especially for his wife at the time, Sarah Brightman.

Aspects of Love (1989) is one of Webber's lesser-known works. After so many costly and spectacular productions, he turned to an intimate chamber play: 17-year-old Alex falls in love with the actress Rose, who becomes involved with Alex's libertine uncle George. Both George and Rose have an affair with the sculptress Giulietta. Years later George falls in love with Alex's 14-year-old daughter Jenny, who meets Giulietta. Prompted primarily by sexual interests, *Aspects of Love* is most definitely not a "musical for children." Webber's score may not be one of his richest but it does offer the hit "Love Changes Everything." Webber at the Dresden state operetta for the German premiere in May 1997 (scene photo).

including the fall of a huge chandelier and a boat trip on the underground lake, as well as awesome sets. Among the better-known songs from the show are "Think of Me," "Wishing You Were Somehow Here Again," and "Music of the Night." *Phantom* gave Webber as composer a chance to expand on his strong classical background, with the sweeping sounds and aesthetics of grand romantic opera. Not long before he had flexed his classical muscles with his *Requiem*, written after *Starlight Express*. The New York premiere of the *Requiem* in 1985 was conducted by Loren Maazel, with Placido Domingo singing the tenor solos.

Sunset Boulevard (1993), as the title suggests, harks back to the Hollywood melodramas of the 1940s and

The German-language version of *Sunset Boulevard*. Instead of selling the stage rights to a licensed buyer, Webber's newly created marketing company, The Really Useful Group, produced the show for the first time in Germany.

1950s. No wonder: The show is based on a masterpiece of this genre, which painted a disillusioned picture of the dream factory. Like Billy Wilder's movie of the same name, the musical *Sunset Boulevard* deals with the doomed comeback attempt of the long-forgotten silent movie star Norma Desmond. The cynical and unsuccessful screenwriter Joe Gillis, who is supposed to help her, moves in with the eccentric diva and lets her support him. Norma disposes of Joe just as she disposed of her ex-producer and ex-husband Max von Mayerling, now demoted to a servant. When Joe refuses to become her lover and attempts to convince her that she will never return to the screen, he meets with disaster. Webber teamed up with Don Black and renowned British dramatist Christopher Hampton to write *Sunset Boulevard*. The music cites the swing sounds of the 1940s and the romantic movie scores of Max

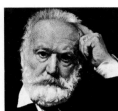

Steiner or Miklos Roszas out of Hollywood's heyday. Glenn Close, known and respected both in Hollywood and on Broadway, played Desmond in the face of some casting controversy, but the casting proved to be a stroke of luck. Indeed, her departure from the show proved that public interest would still seriously wane without a powerful star in the role. In the spring of 1997, *Sunset Boulevard* closed both on Broadway and in the West End. Though a four-year run in London might represent a triumph to most composers, to Webber it was a disappointment not to live up to the slogan for *Cats*—"Now and Forever."

Schoenberg and Boublil

While it cannot accurately be said that any other culture has produced musicals to rival the British or the American traditions, occasionally shows arrive on the scene by what might be called nontraditional routes—that is, originating somewhere other than New York (or sometimes Los Angeles) or London. The works of the French composer-author team Claude-Michel Schoenberg and Alain Boublil also conquered the inter-

national market with operatic, continuous scores, historical subjects, and impressive production values. When an acquaintance gave him a recording of a French musical, Cameron Mackintosh's reaction was skeptical: To him, a French musical appeared to be an oxymoron. But when

Victor Hugo (1802–1885), in his novel *Les Misérables* (The miserable ones), leveled sharp criticism at the social conditions in France during his lifetime.

Les Misérables (scene photo of a German production) plays against the backdrop of the Parisian July revolution of 1830 and the worker riots of 1832–1834. In the center of the wide-ranging action stands the freed convict Jean Valjean, who, after nineteen years of wrongful imprisonment for stealing a loaf of bread, rises to become a socially dedicated factory owner. Pursued by the obsessed gendarme Javer, Valjean and his adopted daughter Cosette flee beneath the streets of Paris. Valjean saves the life of Marius, the revolutionary student beloved by Cosette, but Marius, unaware of what Valjean has done for him, scorns the former convict. They are reconciled shortly before Valjean's death; Valjean dies in the hope of better times and in the assurance that Cosette and Marius are happy.

1978 – today

Kim and Chris in a German production of *Miss Saigon*.

Mackintosh heard the music for *Les Misérables*, he responded with enthusiasm and decided to produce the work, originally mounted in the Paris Palais des Sports, in the West End.

Schoenberg and Boublil were encouraged by Lionel Bart's adaptation of Dickens, *Oliver!*, to tackle Victor Hugo's powerful novel and turn it into a monumental musical play. In 1973 the pair had shown their courage with seemingly unweildy historical subjects with their first work, *La Révolution Française*, which, as the title says, depicted nothing less than the French Revolution. In that production, Schoenberg himself played the part of the guillotined King Louis XVI. Like Webber and Rice's *Jesus Christ Superstar*, *La Révolution Française* first came out as a studio recording. The international success of *Les Misérables* was based on the 1985 London production. Trevor Nunn, flush from his success with *Cats*, directed and coproduced. The show was translated into 14 languages and produced in 19 countries, always according to Nunn's direction and using John Napier's designs. For all the beauty of the spectacle and the intelligent staging, the power of *Les Misérables* lies in Schoenberg's powerful music, which holds the work together, moves it forward, and compensates for the unavoidable ponderousness of Hugo's novel. Unlike some cintinuous-score musicals, which sometimes bridge the gaps between songs with unimaginative recitatives or pedestrian chord sequences, Schoenberg creates a thick atmosphere with his melodic diversity and recurring leitmotifs. His strength lies in emotional ballads like "On My Own" or the swan song of the failed revolution, "Empty Chairs and Empty Tables."

Schoenberg and Boublil's next work was *Miss Saigon*, which, unlike *Les Misérables*, opened first in English in London's West End. *Miss Saigon* tells the tragic love story of an American and a Vietnamese against the background of the Vietnam War, and in the process introduces a series of memorable melodies including "I Still Believe" and "Why God Why?" Boublil and Schoenberg succeeded in balancing melodrama and historical epic, rock rhythms and operatic mellowness, stirring chamber play and large scenic theater, sentiment and special effects—like the landing of a full-size helicopter to carry the last Americans out of the fallen Saigon. Nicholas Hytner's production and Schoenberg's music bind together the expansive shifts in location and time, and hold the audience in emotional thrall. The story is told in constant exchange between aria-like songs and duets, sung and spoken recitative texts, as well as instrumental passages reminiscent of film scores. The composer suggests the Asian setting by approximating Vietnamese instruments using the bassoon or different flutes, without lapsing into folkloristic sound color.

Schoenberg's and Boublil's fourth musical, *Martin Guerre* (1996), contrasts strivings for personal happiness with events in the larger world. Instead of a failing revolution or the Vietnam War, the love story between Bertrande de Rols and Arnaud du Thil overshadows the religious wars in 16th-century France. In favor of a still more self-contained musical setting, Schoenberg dispensed with memorable songs, on which he had relied in the scores of *Les Misérables* and *Miss Saigon*.

In their earnestness and daring to express extreme emotion, the musical dramas of Webber or Schoenberg and Boublil fall in the tradition of the grand romantic operas of composers like Bellini and Meyerbeer, of movie melodramas and of the serious dramatic works of Rodgers and Hammerstein. Not many traces of the jazz and wit of the early American musicals à la

The village idiot in the London production of Schoenberg and Boublil's *Martin Guerre*, based on a true story set in the mid-16th century in the remote Pyrenee village of Artigat. Before a court in Toulouse, a farmer's wife, Bertrande de Rols, explains that the man with whom she has lived for three years is not her husband Martin Guerre, but a swindler named Arnaud du Thil. The defendant insists that he is Martin Guerre, and maintains that Bertrande was forced by her greedy uncle to make her statement, since he was going to inherit a plot of land. The court is predisposed to believe the defendant, when the real Martin Guerre appears. Arnaud du Thil is condemned and executed. This intriguing story was already written by the real-life judge Coras, and served as storyline for the German philosopher Leibniz as well as inspiration for several novels, operas, and movies. The most recent films star actors like Gérard Depardieu or Richard Gere (in *Sommersby*).

1978 – today

163

Kurt Weill and Bertolt Brecht's *Threepenny Opera* did not emerge in a state-subsidized house like most German theater, but was the inaugural production of Ernst Josef Aufricht's Berlin private theater at the Schiffbauerdamm, later the home of Brecht's Berlin ensemble. Photo from the 1931 film starring Weill's wife Lotte Lenya as Jenny.

Poster from the original production of the most successful German musical, *Im Weissen Rössl* (*The White Horse Inn*).

Gershwin or Porter are evident. Comic moments emerge only through scurrilous (and stock literary) figures like the sleezy innkeepers Monsieur and Madame Thénardier in *Les Misérables*. Still, these productions raise a chicken-and-egg sort of question: Since long runs and global marketing are vital to cover the astronomical costs of mounting such elaborate productions, authors and producers are drawn to more timeless, classical subjects—which cross national and cultural boundaries and age well—and averse to contemporary stories or current events.

Noncommercial musicals?

While the success of imports on the Broadway stage shows that Yankee know-how is not the only source of commercial success, it changes little in the theatrical production system: Money still talks. But the musical, as an art form, now has a freshness and legitimacy thanks to the years of experimentation that as often ended in failure as in success. With mainstream Broadway and West End productions competing in a theaterland version of "Can You Top This?," many creative theater artists can't possibly enter the fray—and therefore don't even try. Where once a show produced off Broadway, say, at Joe Papp's Public Theater, or even at regional festivals around the country or around the world, might just "make it" to Broadway, and then might just become a hit and make a name for all involved, many just might not. Then what happens? They do not get recorded; they do not get popularized; often they are not remembered. But experimentation will always be at the heart of musical theater, and this, today, is probably best not judged by the Broadway standards of success. Only one of many possible examples of the simultaneous regionalization and legitimation of musical theater is a program called "CrossCurrents," jointly based in Philadelphia, Pennsylvania, and Cambridge, Massachusetts, self-described as "a major multi-year initiative ... designed to create and sustain a body of new music theater works." Musicals emerging from programs such as this will likely play at repertory stages around the world,

wherever they may originate, and may be, more than any long-run Broadway hit, the artistic future.

Originally a rather kitschy operetta, *Im Weissen Rössl* was revamped and revived into a successful show in 1994.

Musicals off the beaten path

We have now had hits from England and hits from France. Obviously, American artists still apply themselves to musical theater. But where else is the musical alive and well, if anywhere? And if nowhere, why not? As a case in point, let's consider Germany. It may be an exemplar for other cultures; it may also have its own, unique features.

There has been no German counterpart to Schoenberg and Boublil, at least not within Germany. In the 1920s, when the American musical came of age, all the prerequisites for a blooming musical theater were in place. Berlin boasted countless private theaters catering to public tastes. Variety acts and revues were very popular. Two very different works that achieved international success offer evidence that there was indeed a German musical theater environment that—had circumstances been different—might have evolved along a path similar to that of the American scene. When composer Kurt Weill, before he was forced out of his native country, teamed up with playwright Bertolt Brecht, who was a vocal advocate of a brand of theater that through entertainment afforded enlightenment, and favored the use of song to break the illusion

In contrast to the English or French theater, whose forebears Shakespeare and Molière stood firmly within the tradition of people's theater and commercial show business, the German theater has always distinguished between socially relevant art and mere entertainment. The musical—even the operetta—could only have developed in a commercially oriented theater system like the Anglo-American. Germany's publicly funded municipal and national theater, with its educational tradition, has fostered other theatrical forms. That the entertaining musical theater has also doubtless produced works of art does little to change the German "highbrow" opinion that it is an inferior theater form, which still is attached to the musical in Germany.

1978 – today

165

Elisabeth by Michael Kunze and Sylvester Levay is one of the few productions from the German-speaking countries that has been produced in other countries.

Gaudí, a pop musical by Scottish composer Eric Woolfson, premiered in 1993 at the Aachen State Theater. Subsequently the work was marketed to the private sector. Through the story of Catalan architect Antoni Gaudí, *Gaudí* deals with the relationship between art and commerce: an apt theme for a musical.

1978 – today

of the stage action and keep the audience ever aware of the artificial nature of the play, they enjoyed great success with their reworking of *The Beggar's Opera* into *The Threepenny Opera* (1928). Like the early operettas of Offenbach, Weill and Brecht employed sharp, timely criticism with popular musical forms. In no time at all, *The Threepenny Opera* was playing on the stages of countless German municipal theaters. Songs like the "Ballad of Mack the Knife" ("Mackie Messer") and "Pirate Jenny" became popular around the world. *The Threepenny Opera* was brought to New York in 1933, but it was not really successful in the home of the modern musical until Marc Blitzstein produced a concert version in 1954, conducted by Leonard Bernstein. In 1977, Broadway celebrated Brecht and Weill's *Happy End*, which had brought to life the characters from Damon Runyon's stories a good 20 years before *Guys and Dolls*.

And Brecht and Weill were not alone as authors of German musicals. Today, some of the "singspiels" and other German shows have been mined for fresh material to feed both London and New York. With the international musical marketing pattern in place today, great musical productions like *Das Weisse Rössl* are being marketed worldwide; this particular show was once produced in London under the title *The White Horse Inn*, and transferred from there to New York in 1936—a path not unlike that of *Irma La Douce* and *Les Misérables*. But that was a long time ago, and in the meanwhile …

As with so many aspects of German life, the Nazis swiftly put an end to any cultural blossoming this brief period of German musical theater might have produced. Between the Nazis' strict control (and patrol) of the arts and media, and the forced emigration or elimination of so many Jewish musicians, performers, and writers, the hole in German theater was too great. While circumstances in the United States were converging to bring forth the musical theater, in Germany they converged to close it down for too many years. Not much would happen until well after the war.

For a long time, it was suggested that one reason the musical flourished in England and the United States, but not in Germany, had to do with the innate properties of the German language. English, it was asserted, was more suited to expressing emotion and lends itself to a variety of voices and inflections. German, on the other hand, was a drag on the tongue—ill-suited to the flexibility of jazzy or modern pop rhythms. But a German translation of Cole Porter's *Kiss Me, Kate*, by Gunter Neumann, and somewhat later the translations of many contemporary musicals, including those of Andrew Lloyd Webber, by Michael Kunze put that excuse to rest. A more palatable explanation for the relative diluteness of German-language musicals being produced in Germany may lie in the different theater system. Germany has a structure of state theaters that are generally willing to take risks with new musicals, but the

The Black Rider: Producer and stage designer Robert Wilson created severe, stark silhouetted pictures, reminiscent of German Expressionist silent movies such as Murnau's *Nosferatu* or Wiene's *Caligari*.

production process is markedly different from the American or the British process. Before a show opens on Broadway, it has usually been well tried elsewhere—either in London, or in out-of-town tryouts, or on a record. This gives the producers an opportunity to develop and refine the work so that when it has its long-anticipated opening night, it is a polished,

Volker Ludwig's *Linie 1* celebrated its opening in April 1986; now entering its twelfth season, it continues to play to a full house.

1978 – today

167

In the 1980s, the American book musical lost more and more ground to the grand-scale British imports. American composer Maury Yeston almost abandoned his own *Phantom of the Opera* project in 1985 when he learned that Andrew Lloyd Webber was also working on an adaptation of the novel by Gaston Leroux. Yeston's version—no pop opera, but a musical in the classic Broadway tradition—premiered in 1991 in Houston, Texas.

Duke Ellington's melodies made up the 1981 revue *Sophisticated Ladies*.

professional production. An opening night in Germany is truly an opening night: Even large-scale commercial productions meet the public for the first time at their premiere, with reviewers in attendance. There are no second chances and the first performance can quite easily be the last.

The first German performance of *Cats* in Hamburg in 1986 cultivated a devoted following for musicals among German theater goers. This could not have happened if there weren't already something of a musical culture in place. One notable contribution of original German musical theater was *The Black Rider*, produced in 1990 in Hamburg at the Thalia Theater. The show was a collaborative effort, ironically, by three Americans—drama producer and artist Robert Wilson, song writer Tom Waits, and Beat poet William S. Burroughs. Like the legendary extravaganza *The Black Crook*, *The Black Rider* is based on the motif of the marksman's contest. William must prove in a shooting contest that he is worthy of the forester's daughter, Käthchen. He makes a pact with the devil, but his last bullet kills his beloved. The Wilson, Waits, and Burroughs trio followed the success of *The Black Rider* with *Alice*, based on *Alice in Wonderland*.

The most important German musical since *The Threepenny Opera* is *Linie 1*, written by Volker Ludwig, director of a theater group in Berlin. Ludwig began writing a nonmusical drama, then

composed a series of song texts for scenes and characters, performed by Birger Heymann and members of the band No Ticket. Ludwig took his inspiration from the Berlin subway-line 1, which runs from the prosperous West of Berlin to the once poor, but enticing part called Kreuzberg. The show is a mixture of deft realism and utopian hopes, caberet-like jokes and sympathetic character pictures; it follows the classic pattern of musicals and yet is unmistakably German.

The American Book Musical

Nostalgia and navel gazing

For want of sufficient new shows suitable for Broadway, the trend of staging revivals has only gained momentum since the 1960s. Where once, in the halcyon days of the New York theater district, only undisputed masterpieces were honored with revival, in recent years even relatively unknown musicals have come out of hiding. And because Broadway reveres its traditions, there have also been a slew of nostalgic revues devoted to the music of some individual or fashion: *Ain't Misbehavin'* (1978) showcased the music of pianist and composer Fats Waller; Gershwin's early musicals were reworked for *My One and Only* (1983) and *Crazy for You* (1992); Jerry Herman was remembered in *Jerry's Girls* (1985); Bob Fosse's choreography was celebrated in *Dancin'* (1978); Jerome Robbins was the focus of *Broadway* (1989); and the list could in fact go on almost ad infinitum.

Artists and crises

Many new musicals examined different aspects of show business. Cy Coleman's turbulent relationship comedy *On the 20th Century* (1978) takes place on a train en route from Chicago to New York and recounts a theater producer's efforts to win back his star ex-wife by any means. *Barnum* (1980) is the life story of the showman

Ann Reinking in Bob Fosse's *Dancin'*.

That Cy Coleman's *City of Angels* was also seen in Germany is a credit to the Heilbronner Theater, which had previously made its mark with German premieres of Sondheim's *Into the Woods* and *Assassins*, as well as Willy Russell's *Blood Brothers*.

1978 – today

Phineas Taylos Barnum (1810–1891), who as the "Prince of Humbug" began with a freak show and ended up presenting "The Greatest Show on Earth" in his three-ring-circus.

With *City of Angels* (1980), Coleman succeeded with a loving tribute to Hollywood's "film noir" and to authors like Raymond Chandler and Dashiell Hammett. Set in the "City of Angels," Los Angeles, where authors like Chandler, Hammett, F. Scott Fitzgerald, and William Faulkner worked as contract screenwriters for the motion picture industry in the 1940s, the show featured David Zippel's elegant and smug song lyrics, while Coleman's music evoked the swing sound of the era. After writing about theater, the circus, and the dream factory of Hollywood, Colemen, with lyricists Betty Comden and Adolph Green, turned to the legendary revues of Florenz Ziegfeld in *Will Rogers' Follies* about the cowboy-actor and comedian Will Rogers, who appeared in many

Nine (1982): Anita Morris's seductive "Call from the Vatican" was too hot for the broadcast of the Tony Awards. Shortly before airing, the telephone sex song was removed from the program.

of Ziegfeld's productions in the 1920s. In what might have been an expression of national partisanship among New York critics eager to bolster original American musicals or nostalgic for the flavor of the conventional American production, *Will Rogers' Follies* actually won the Tony Award for best musical of the season, beating out *Miss Saigon*. The public, however, still seemed to prefer the music dramas of

1978 – today

Schoenberg and Boublil over the American book musicals.

Like *City of Angels*, Maury Yeston's *Nine* is about a film maker in a creative and emotional crisis; like Cy Coleman's earlier work *Sweet Charity*, *Nine* was based on a film by Federico Fellini. The show is about film director Guido, who, one week before the actions begins, cannot decide whether he should make a spaghetti western, a biblical epic, or an earnest documentary. This catapults him into a midlife crisis. In the sung overture, he conducts an orchestra of the women in his life, but things get out of control. His wife Luisa is no longer willing to tolerate his philandering; his demanding mistress Carla puts him at ease with erotic phone calls. He suddenly decides that the star of his earlier films, Claudia, is in fact the great, unfulfilled love of his life, his producer pressures him for a decision, and a dreaded French film critic gives him her not exactly flattering opinion. The action follows the fantasies and "stream of consciousness" of the protagonist. In a vision, Guido sees himself as a child again and his mother appears to him as a prostitute, from whom he seeks to discover the secrets of love. Inspired by Claudia to do a film about Casanova, he throws himself into his work and disrupts all his

relationships. Finally wiping his slate clean, he knows that Luisa is his true love. Yeston's music spans everything from jazzy show songs to operetta arias to baroque choral settings, citing vibrant French music hall atmosphere and Nino Rota's scores for Fellini's movies. Producer and choreographer Tommy Tune decided to cast the

Maury Yeston's *Grand Hotel* (1985) reworked an older musical by Robert Wright and George Forrest.

Big River became the surprise hit of the 1985 season, largely due to Roger Miller's fresh music, which ranged from country and western to blues and gospel.

1978 – today

171

Parallels between the story of *Dreamgirls* and the true story of Diana Ross and the Supremes stirred up considerable emotion. The show's manager replaced heavy-set lead singer Effie Melody White with another performer who looked more like the desired glamorous type. Unlike the real Florence Ballard, who died in poverty at the age of 32, Effie breaks through with a solo career and realizes ten years later when performing with her former partners that she is in fact happier than they are.

musical entirely with women (with the exception of Raul Julia as Guido), and with a stylized black and white set and Yeston's original music, *Nine* turned into an extraordinary theatrical event.

Soul and country

Like *A Chorus Line*, Michael Bennett's *Dreamgirls* (1981) also plays as a "work in progress." Influenced by the story of the Supremes, *Dreamgirls* follows the career of a female soul trio from the Apollo Theater in Harlem all the way to Las Vegas. Michael Bennett's staging keeps things in constant motion, and music and dancing dominate the evening. While Henry Krieger's music brought the sounds of Motown to the musical stage, the country and western sounds of folk singer Roger Miller came to Broadway in 1985. The producer team Rocco and Heidi Landsmann persuaded Miller, who by his own report had only seen one musical, to write the songs for an adaptation of Mark Twain's *Huckleberry Finn* called *Big River*. William Hauptmann's libretto was faithful to Twain's novel and maintained as far as possible the perspective of the subjective narrator (the boy Huck).

Rent

Since its Broadway premiere on April 29, 1996, Jonathan Larson's *Rent* has shown a 102 percent profit. It is not uncommon to have to wait in line for six to twelve hours at the box office to get tickets for the show a month later. The 99-seat New York Theater Workshop where *Rent* originally played off Broadway was constantly bursting at its seams, especially after word of mouth and the first euphoric critics called it "the hottest show in town"—a new *Hair*. *Rent* was soon hailed as the rebirth of the American musical, showered with Tony Awards and given the Pulitzer Prize for drama. Unfortunately, the author Jonathan Larson did not live to see these honors and the triumph of his portrait of a lost generation. A few days before his first work played in public, Larson died suddenly. *Rent* ostensibly follows the format of the successful European productions: Through a recitative accompanied by electric guitar, the lively rock songs, duets, and ensemble numbers are strung together. Moreover, *Rent* is a modern version of Puccini's opera *La Bohème* and, as such,

purports to be an authentic portrait of urban life at the end of the 20th century. Larson, who supported himself as a waiter while working on the project, knew his subject matter from his own experience. His Bohemians are performance artists, film makers, rock musicians, and transvestites struggling for success and survival in New York's East Village. Mimi is dying not of consumption but of AIDS. The ballad "One Song Glory" expresses the hopes of the guitar player Roger to write a hit before he dies—a macabre parallel to Larson's own fate. But the characters in *Rent* face grinding anxiety over AIDS, poverty, hunger, the search for drugs, and homelessness with stubborn optimism and courage. Larson's music is a mixture of skillful hard rock and quiet ballads, soul and salsa, gospel and reggae.

Jonathan Larson's *Rent* shows what a musical at the end of the 20th century can offer: reality, life, energy, authenticity, enthusiasm, and genuine feeling.

The Mystery of Edwin Drood. Rupert Holmes wrote the music, book, and lyrics for this adaptation of Charles Dickens's fragment of a novel by the same name. The novelist died before he could complete his work and resolve the mystery around the disappeared, probably murdered title figure. The musical, patterned after a 19th century British music hall show, ends asking the audience who the murderer was. Depending on the audience's decision, the cast plays out one of a number of endings.

1978 – today

1997

Despite ever climbing ticket prices, Broadway is prospering. The audience demand and, with it, profits climb from year to year. *Rent* is not the

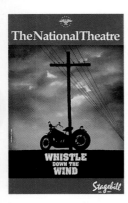

The tryouts for *Whistle Down the Wind* still proclaimed that Andrew Lloyd Webber's new musical, directed by Harold Prince, would open on Broadway in early 1997. Set in a rural Louisiana town in the year 1959, the story deals with a young girl, who converts a foreigner hiding in the family barn to Jesus.

only production turning a profit: In May 1997, 22 musicals were running on Broadway—more than at almost any time in the past. The exuberant *Bring in 'da Noise, Bring in 'da Funk*, which tells (in song and dance) the history of African Americans from their abduction from Africa into slavery to the rap music of the 1990s, inspired audiences nightly in 1997 with an entire evening of artistic choreography. Its star Savion Glover was celebrated by the critics as a "new Fred Astaire."

While the British productions *The Phantom of the Opera* and *Miss Saigon* were still playing to full houses and *Cats* broke the record for longest running musical set by *A Chorus Line* in the summer of 1997, the press declared that Andrew Lloyd Webber's success was on the wane: *Sunset Boulevard* closed much sooner than expected in the West End and on Broadway. The Broadway premiere planned for April 1997 of Webber's newest musical, *Whistle Down the Wind*, was postponed indefinitely after being raked over the coals by critics. Maury Yeston, Cy Coleman, and Kander and Ebb all prepared new book musicals in spring 1997 to compete with European imports. While Yeston's extravagant production *Titanic* used the disaster on the luxury liner as a take off point for oblique social criticism, Coleman's *The Life* follows in the footsteps of *Guys and Dolls*, affectionately portraying the world of hookers and pimps around Times Square during the 1970s. And, after their international successes *Cabaret* and *Chicago*, John Kander and Fred Ebb again depict a bygone era. *Steel Pier*, set during the Great Depression, revolves around a dance marathon in a ballroom in Atlantic City. In the spring of 1997, seven years after its opening at the Houston Alley Theatre and after a nationwide tour, Frank Wildhorn and Leslie Bricusse brought their show *Jekyll and Hyde* to Broadway. The adaptation of Robert Louis

Stevenson's novel often departs from the original as a sung-through music drama in the European mold. The exaggerated rock opera about the experiments of the affable Dr. Jekyll, whose darker side is animated in the impulsive Hyde, calls on songs like the gloomy Faustian ballad "I Need to Know," the jubilant hymn "This Is the Moment," or the rhythmic-folkloric "Bring on the Men." Other extravaganzas with Wildhorn's music have already appeared as concept albums or been announced, among them a musical drama called *The Civil War: An American Musical* and *Svengali*, another adaptation of the classic Victorian novel.

Maury Yeston's *Titanic* was the big winner at the 1997 Tony Awards.

Rent has demonstrated that the musical is still vital at the end of the millenium. Never has the range of themes and forms been so great, never has the palette of musical expression been so expansive. Which predictions may come true—will the American musical, like the operetta, congeal into convention and cliché or will it blossom into a new renaissance; has Andrew Lloyd Webber's stint at the top of the heap come to an end; is *Cats* really here "Now and Forever;" where will the next foreign musical imports come from—will there be a Russian musical, a Latvian musical, a Japanese or a Spanish or a Chinese musical? Only time will tell.

Jekyll and Hyde (CD cover): After the European model, the young American composer Frank Wildhorn and his more experienced British lyricist Leslie Bricusse first recorded over 60 songs that served as the basis for the stage work.

1978 – today

Glossary

Glossary

Act: A major section of a work for spoken or musical theater. Most musicals, like Mozart's opera *The Magic Flute*, consist of two acts with an intermission. Unlike some classic drama and opera, this subdivision is purely practical, rather than structural, in nature.

Angels (also **Backers**): Financiers for private-sector theater productions on Broadway or in London's West End.

Arrangement: Adaptation or reworking of a piece of music for a certain instrumental and vocal ensemble.

Audition: The tryout of singing and dancing musical performers, who apply for a specific role or for a part in the ensemble. Auditions are announced by the producer; as a rule the musical director, producer, and choreographer, and often also the composer and author make the casting decisions. An audition is the center of the story of the musical *A Chorus Line*.

Backers: See **Angels**

Ballad: A song usually in simple form, with which a story is told.

Ballad opera: A parodistic, lighthearted musical comedy with popular songs that developed in 18th century England; first and best-known example is *The Beggar's Opera* by Gay and Pepusch.

Book musicals: Classic American musicals with spoken dialogue, song, and dance numbers integrated into the action, and a serious plot.

Can-can: Dance made popular after 1830 in Paris, in fast two-quarter time, consisting of a line of women kicking and lifting their skirts in unison.

Choreography: Delineated sequence of steps and movements of a dance.

Chorus: The dancing and singing ensemble of a musical production whose members have few or no solo parts or dialogue.

Dance captain: Staff member who works with the choreographer, rehearsing the dance numbers and movement with the soloists and chorus.

Duet: Piece of music for two singing voices.

Encore: Repeat of a song in response to audience acclaim.

Folk opera: A popular form of musical theater with elements of classical opera (orchestra, classically trained voices), appeals to a wide public and is judged on both artistic and commercial grounds. Given impetus by George Bizet's *Carmen*, the American theater produced George Gershwin's *Porgy and Bess*, Kurt Weill's *Street Scene*, Frank Loesser's *The Most Happy Fella*, and Leonard Bernstein's *Candide* to lead the musical into "American folk opera."

Jazz dance: Like jazz music, a dance form from African-American culture. In contrast to the whole body technique of classical European ballet, jazz dance is marked by polycentrism: Each limb is isolated and moves independently of other body parts. The pelvis is the center of movement.

Leitmotif: Musical theme that returns throughout a work to refer to a specific character, event, or idea.

Libretto: The script of a work of musical theater, with dialogue as well as song lyrics.

Modern dance: American stage dancing, as distinct from classical ballet. Modern dance experienced its peak in the late 1920s and 1930s; its most important representative was Martha Graham. Contrary to the severe rules of the ballet, modern dance uses free and subjective movement with dramatic expression.

Musical: Adjectival short form of the original designation musical comedy, later also a musical play or musical drama. Musicals developed in the United States with the fusion of popular musical forms, dance, and entertaining theater.

Operetta (French "little opera"): The European tradition originating from

Glossary

musical stage shows with exchanges of spoken dialogue, instrumental and song numbers, choruses and ballets, catchy melodies and a light-hearted plot.

Score: The notation of a piece of music showing all instrumental and vocal parts.

Preview: Public performance of a play before the official premiere, in the theater where the show will run.

Recitative: Declamatory style of singing, sometimes accompanied by orchestra and sometimes just by keyboard, which imitates natural speech rhythms and intonation. In operas and occasionally also in musicals (e.g., *Rent*), recitatives bridge the gaps between sung musical numbers.

Show stoppers: Popular music number, which causes the public to applaud so furiously that the performance has to stop temporarily, possibly to allow for an encore.

Syncopations: Rhythm characteristic of jazz, in which offbeats are emphasized.

Tap dance: Dance performed in shoes with metal "taps" on the soles that produce percussive sounds to the rhythm of the dance. Its roots are in the Irish Jig, the English clog dance, and also in African clog dances, which were brought by slaves to America. In contrast to the European forms, the African tap dances were very syncopated. In 1848 the black tap dancer Juba had made a hit in London. His fans included Queen Victoria. Well-known tap dancers include Bill "Bojangles" Robinson and Fred Astaire, one of the first successful white tap dancers.

Timbre: The tone quality of a singing voice or a musical instrument, sometimes called "tone color."

Tryouts: Test performances of a new musical, which can still be revised considerably according to public reactions. The tryouts for Broadway productions occur in the provinces, which means all American cities besides New York.

West End: The theater district in London, near Piccadilly Circus, Trafalgar Square, and the Strand in the center of London. Comparable to New York's theater district, Broadway.

Selected Discography

Selected Discography
(arranged by composer)

OBC = Original Broadway Cast
OLC = Original London Cast
L = London Cast
NY = New York Cast
dt. = German Production
Film = Film Soundtrack
S = Studio Production
C = Concert Production

All information refers to CDs

Richard Adler/Jerry Ross
Damn Yankees (OBC) RCA Victor 3948-2-RG
The Pajama Game (OBC) Columbia CK 32606
B. Andersson/B. Ulvaeus
Chess (S) RCA PD 70500 (2)
Harold Arlen
House of Flowers (OBC) Sony Music Special Products A-2320
Jamaica (OBC) RCA 68041
St. Louis Woman (OBC) EMI 764662
The Wizard of Oz (Film) CBS Special Products 45356
Lionel Bart
Blitz! (OLC) EMI CDP 7-97470-2
Oliver! (OLC) Deram 820 590-2
Irving Berlin
Annie Get Your Gun! (OBC) MCA 10047
Call Me Madam (1995) Koch DRG 94761
Louisiana Purchase (USA 1996) Koch DRG 94766
Leonard Bernstein
West Side Story (OBC) Columbia 9CK-32603

Wonderful Town (OBC) MCA 10050
Marc Blitzstein
The Cradle Will Rock (L 1985) Colosseum TER 1105
Jerry Bock
Fiddler on the Roof (OBC) RCA RD-87060 QA
Fiorello! (OBC) Capitol 92052
She Loves Me (OBC) Polydor 831 968-2
Leslie Bricusse/A. Newley
Stop the World – I Want to Get Off (S 1997) Colosseum TER 34.1226
Nacio Herb Brown
Singin' in the Rain (Film) CBS CDCBS-70282
Singin' in the Rain (L 1984) Colosseum 34.5453
George M. Cohan
George M! (OBC) Columbia CK-3200
Cy Coleman
Barnum (OBC) Columbia CK-36576
City of Angels (OBC) Columbia CK 46067
I Love my Wife (OBC) DRG CDRG 6109
The Life (S) RCA 09026680012
Little Me (OBC) RCA Victor 09026-61482-2
Seesaw (OBC) DRG CDRG-6108
Sweet Charity (OBC) Columbia CK-2900
The Will Rogers Follies (OBC) Columbia CK-48606
Noel Coward
Bitter Sweet (L 1988) TER CD 2-1160
Sail Away (OBC) Capitol 64759

Noel Gay
Me and My Girl (L 1985) Manhattan Records CDP 7-46393-2
George Gershwin
Crazy For You (OBC) Broadway Angel CDC 7546182
Girl Crazy (S) Elektra Nonesuch 9-79250-2
Let 'Em Eat Cake + Of Thee I Sing (S) CBS M2K 42522
My One and Only (OBC 1983) Atlantic 801110-2
Porgy and Bess (USA 1996) Dorian 90223
Porgy and Bess (Louis Armstrong/Ella Fitzgerald) Verve 810 040-2
Strike Up the Band (S) Elektra Nonesuch 7559-79273-2
Clark Gesner
You're a Good Man, Charlie Brown (OBC) Polydor 820 262-2
Dan Goggin
Nunsense (OBC) DRG Records CDSBL 12589
Marvin Hamlisch
A Chorus Line (OBC) Columbia CK-33581
A Chorus Line (Film) Casablanca/Polygram 826 655-2Q
The Goodbye Girl (OBC) IRS 6376102
They're Playing Our Song (OBC) Polygram 826 240-2
Jerry Herman
La Cage Aux Folles (OBC) RCA BD-84824
La Cage Aux Folles (dt.) Polydor 829646-2
Hello, Dolly! (OBC) RCA Victor 3814-2-RG
Mack and Mabel (K) First Night Records Cast CD 13

Selected Discography

Mame (OBC) Columbia CK-3000
Milk and Honey (OBC) RCA 61997

Birger Heymann
Linie 1 (dt.) Polydor 831 219-2

Rupert Holmes
The Mystery of Edwin Drood (OBC) PolyGram VSD-5597

Jim Jacobs/Warren Casey
Grease (OBC) Polydor 827 548-2
Grease (Film) Polydor 817 988-2

John Kander
Cabaret (Film) MCA 250 428-2
Cabaret (OBC) Columbia CK-3040 oder CBS CD-70273
Chicago (NY 1996) RCA 09026-68727-2
Kiss of the Spiderwoman (OBC) IMS 314526526
The Rink (OBC) Polydor 823 125-2
Woman of the Year (OBC) Bay Cities BCD-3008
Zorba (NY 1983) RCA RCD1-4732

Jerome Kern
Music in the Air (L 1951) AEI CD 026
Roberta (S) Sony Musical Special Products A-7030
Show Boat (S) EMI CDS 7 49108-2
Very Good Eddie (NY) DRG CDRG 6100

Henry Krieger
Dreamgirls (OBC) Geffen Records 2007-2

Sylvester Levay
Elisabeth (dt., Vienna) Polydor 513 792-2

Burton Lane
Finian's Rainbow (OBC) Columbia 4062

On a Clear Day You Can See Forever (OBC) RCA 60820

Jonathan Larson
Rent (OBC) Dreamworks DRD 50003

Mitch Leigh
Man of La Mancha (OBC) MCA MCAD-1672

Frank Loesser
Guys and Dolls (OBC) MCA Classics MCAD-10301
How to Succeed in Business Without Really Trying (OBC) RCA 60352-2-RG
The Most Happy Fella (OBC) Sony Broadway S2K-48010
Where's Charley? (OLC) Capitol 65071

Frederick Loewe
Brigadoon (L 1988) First Night FNC CD 16
Camelot (OBC) Columbia CK-32602
Gigi (Film) CBS CD-70277
My Fair Lady (OBC) Columbia 5090
My Fair Lady (dt.) Philips 8212 651-2
Paint Your Wagon (OBC) RCA Victor 60243

Galt MacDermot
Dude (OBC) Original Cast 9499
Hair (OBC) RCA Victor BD-89667
Hair (dt.) Polydor 833 103-2

Henry Mancini
Victor Victoria (OBC) Philips 446919

Alan Menken
The Beauty and the Beast (OBC) PolyGram 523597
Little Shop of Horrors (S) Geffen 924 125-2

Roger Miller
Big River (OBC) MCAD 6147

Richard O'Brien
The Rocky Horror Picture Show (Film) Ode ODE CD-1032

Cole Porter
Anything Goes (L 1989) First Night FNC 018
Can-Can (OBC) Capitol 92064
High Society (L) EMI CDP 7 46777-2 (CD-SCX 6707)
Kiss Me, Kate (S 1996) Rough Trade 93902122
Kiss Me, Kate (dt., 1989) Cora 1020
Out of this World (C 1995) DRG Records 94764
Silk Stockings (OBC) RCA Victor 1102-2-RG

Richard Rodgers
Allegro (OBC) RCA 52758
Babes in Arms (S) New World Records NW 386-2
The Boys from Syracuse (NY 1963) EMI 764695
Carousel (NY 1994) EMI 55519924
Flower Drum Song (OBC) Columbia CK-2009
I Remember Mama (S) Colosseum TER 1102
The King and I (OBC) MCA 10049
Me and Juliet (OBC) RCA 61480
No Strings (OBC) EMI 764694
Oklahoma! (OBC) MCA 10046
On Your Toes (NY 1954) MCA 11575
Pal Joey (NY 1995) DRG 94763
Pipe Dream (OBC) RCA 61481

Selected Discography

The Sound of Music
(OBC) CBS CDCBS-70212
South Pacific (OBC)
Columbia CK-32604
Sigmund Romberg
*The Student Prince in
Heidelberg* (S) &TER
34.1172
Harold Rome
Destry Rides Again (L
1982) Colosseum CDTER
1034
Fanny (OBC) RCA
09026680742
Pins and Needles (S
1962) Columbia 57380
Wish You Were Here
(OBC) RCA
09026683262
Willy Russell
Blood Brothers (L) Legacy
Records LLMCD-3007
Harvey Schmidt
The Fantasticks (OBC)
Polydor 821 943-2
I Do! I Do! (OBC) RCA
Victor 1128-2-RC
110 in the Shade (OBC)
RCA Victor 1085-2-RG
Claude-Michel Schönberg
Martin Guerre (OLC)
Polydor 537 263
Les Misérables (French
version) First Night Rec-
ords Encore CD 6
Les Misérables (OLC) First
Night Records Encore CD 1
Miss Saigon (OLC)
Geffen 7599-24271-2
La Révolution Française
(French) Vogue VG 651
600146
Stephen Schwartz
Godspell (OBC) Arista
8304
Pippin (OBC) Motown
MCD 06186 MD
Stephen Sondheim
Anyone Can Whistle
(1995) Sony SMIS 67224

Assassins (OBC) RCA
Victor 60737-2-RC
Company (L 1996)
Colosseum CastCD-57
Follies (OBC) EMI 764
666
*A Funny Thing Happened
on the Way to the Forum*
(OBC) Bay Cities BCD-
3002
Into the Woods (OBC)
RCA Victor RD-86796 QA
A Little Night Music (OBC)
Columbia CK-32265
Marry Me a Little (OBC)
RCA Victor 7142-2-RC
Merrily We Roll Along
(OBC) RCA RCD1-5840
Pacific Overtures (OBC)
RCA RCD1 4407
Passion (OBC) EMI
55525123
*Sunday in the Park with
George* (OBC) RCA
RCD1-5042
Sweeney Todd (OBC)
RCA Red Seal 3379-2-RC
Charles Strouse
Annie (F) Columbia CK-
38000
Bye Bye Birdie (OBC)
Columbia 2025
The Golden Boy (OBC)
EMI 766024
Jule Styne
Do Re Mi (OBC) RCA
61994
Funny Girl (OBC) Capitol
CDP 7 46634 2
Gentlemen Prefer Blondes
(NY 1995) Koch DRG
94762
Gypsy (OBC) Columbia
CK-32607
High Button Shoes (OBC)
RCA CAD1-457
Peter Pan (OBC, more
songs by Mark Charlap)
RCA Victor GD-83762-QH

Arthur Sullivan
HMS Pinafore (1987)
Bellaphon Show CD 22
The Mikado (1986)
Bellaphon Show CD 5
The Pirates of Penzance
(S) Bellaphon Show CD 10
The Yeoman of the Guard
(S) Telarc 80404
Pete Townsend
Quadrophenia (S)
PolyGram 531 971
Tommy (S, The Who 1969)
Polydor 800 077-2
Tommy (OBC 1993) RCA
0902661874
Tom Waits
The Black Rider (S, Tom
Waits) Ariola 2116822
Harry Warren
42nd Street (OBC) RCA
BD-83891
Andrew Lloyd Webber
Aspects of Love (OLC)
Polydor 841 126-2
By Jeeves (L 1996)
Polydor 533 187-2
Cats (OLC) Polydor 817
810-2
Evita (OLC) MCA 250 578-2
Evita (Film) Warner Bros.
9362-46450
Jesus Christ Superstar (S)
MCA DMCX-501
*Joseph and the Amazing
Technicolor Dreamcoat* (L
1991) Polydor 511 130-2
The Phantom of the Opera
(OLC) Polydor 831 273-2
Song and Dance (OLC)
Polydor 843617-2
Starlight Express (OLC)
Polydor 821 597-2
Starlight Express (dt.) CBS
462585
Sunset Boulevard (OBC)
Polydor 527 241-2
Kurt Weill
Die Dreigroschenoper
(dt.) Polymedia 847 515

Selected Discography

The Threepenny Opera (L 1995) Colosseum CDTER 1227

Happy End (dt.) Capriccio 60015-1

Johnny Johnson (S) Polydor 831 384-2

Lady in the Dark (S) Sony Classical MHK 62869

Lost in the Stars (OBC) MCA Classics MCAD-10302

One Touch of Venus (OBC) MCA Classics MCAD-11354

Street Scene (English National Opera 1989) TER Classics CD 1185-2

Frank Wildhorn

Jekyll & Hyde (S) TIS 82723

The Scarlet Pimpernel (S) EMI 7543972

Meredith Willson

The Music Man (OBC) Capitol CDP 7 46633 2

The Unsinkable Molly Brown (OBC) Capitol 92054

Sandy Wilson

The Boy Friend (L 1984) TER CD 1095

Eric Woolfson

Gaudi (1995) WEA 063102892

Maury Yeston

Grand Hotel (OBC) BMG 0902 661 3276 5

Nine (OBC) CBS CK-38325

The Phantom of the Opera (S) Ariola 2661660

Vincent Youmans

Hit the Deck (Film) EMI MGM 15

No, No, Nanette (NY 1971) IRS 3056302

Selected Bibliography

Selected Bibliography

Bailey, Leslie:
The Gilbert and Sullivan Book, London 1952.

Banfield, Stephen:
Sondheim's Broadway Musicals, Ann Arbor (MI) 1993.

Behr, Edward and Steyn, Mark:
The Story of Miss Saigon, London/New York 1991.

Bell, Marty:
Broadway Stories: A Backstage Journey trough Musical Theatre, New York 1993.

Berggren, Laurence:
As Thousands Cheer—The Life of Irving Berlin, London 1990.

Bloom, Ken:
American Song: The Complete Musical Theatre Companion 1900–1984, New York 1985.

Casper, Joseph Andrew:
Vincente Minelli and the Musical Film, South Brunswick 1977.

Cohan, George M.:
Twenty Years on Broadway, New York 1925.

Corey, Glenn M. (ed.):
Musical Theatre in America, Westport (CT) 1984.

Engel, Lehman:
Planning and Producing the Musical Show, New York 1966.

Ewen, D.:
The Story of Jerome Kern, New York 1953

Farber, Donald C.:
The Amazing Story of The Fantasticks, Secaucus (NJ) 1991.

Farnsworth, Marjorie:
The Ziegfeld Follies: A History in Text and Pictures, New York 1956.

Feuer, Jane:
The Hollywood Musical, Bloomington (IN) 1982.

Friedland, Michael:
Irving Berlin, New York 1974.

Gänzl, Kurt:
The Encyclopedia of the Musical Theatre, Oxford 1994.

Gottfried, Martin:
Broadway Musicals, New York 1993.
Sondheim, New York 1993.

Green, Stanley:
Broadway Musicals, Show by Show, London 1987.
Encyclopedia of the Musical Film, New York 1981.
Ring Bells! Sing Songs! Broadway Musicals of the 30's, New York 1971.
Rodgers and Hammerstein, New York 1980.
The World of Musical Comedy, South Brunswick 1976.

Greenberger, Howard:
The Off-Broadway Experience, Eaglewood Cliffs (NJ) 1971.

Hewitt, Bernard:
Theatre USA 1668–1957, New York 1957.

Hischak, Thomas S.:
Word Crazy: Broadway Lyricists from Cohan to Sondheim, New York 1991.

Horn, Barbara L.:
The Age of Hair, New York 1991.

Kimball, Robert (ed.):
Cole, New York 1971.

Kreuger, Miles:
Show Boat: The Story of a Classical Musical, New York 1977.

Kronenberger, Louis and Goberman, Max (ed.):
John Gay: The Beggar's Opera, New York 1962.

Lees, Gene:
Inventing Champagne: The Worlds of Lerner and Loewe, New York 1990.

Lerner, Alan Jay:
The Musical Theatre: A Celebration, New York 1986.

MacGovern, Dennis:
Sing Out, Louise!, New York 1993.

Mandelbaum, Ken:
A Chorus Line and the Musicals of Michael Bennett, New York 1989.
Not Since Carrie: 40 Years of Broadway Flops, New York 1991.

Martin, Gerald:
American Operetta: From HMS Pinafore to Sweeney Todd, New York 1981.

Morddens, Ethan:
Rodgers & Hammerstein, New York 1993.

Rodgers, Richard:
The Rodgers and Hart Sound Book, New York 1951.

Rodgers, Richard and Hammerstein, Oscar:
Six Plays (Oklahoma!, Carousel, Allegro, South Pacific, The King and I, Me and Juliet), New York 1959.

Root, Deane L.:
American Popular Stage Music (1860–1880), Ann Arbor (MI) 1981.

Selected Bibliography and Index of Names

Salem, James M.:
A Guide to Critical Reviews, Washington DC 1988.

Schwartz, Charles:
Cole Porter, New York 1977.

Sennett, Ted:
Hollywood Musicals, New York 1981.

Sheward, David:
It's a Hit!—The Backstage Book of Longest-Running Broadway Shows 1884–1994, New York 1994.

The Shubert Archive (ed.):
The Shuberts of Broadway, New York 1990.

Shurtleff, Michael:
Audition, New York 1978.

Sobel, Bernard:
A Pictorial History of Vaudeville, New York 1961.

Suskin, Stephen:
Opening Night on Broadway, New York 1990.

Swain, Joseph P.:
The Broadway Musical: A Critical and Musical Survey, New York 1991.

Toll, Robert C.:
The Entertainment Machine, Oxford etc. 1982.

Wilk, Max:
OK!: The Story of Oklahoma!, New York 1993.

Wittke, Carl:
Tambo and Bones. A History of the American Minstrel Stage, Durham (NC) 1930.

Wodehouse; P.G. and Bolton, Guy:
Bring on the Girls. Life in Musical Comedy, New York 1953.

Index of Names

Index of Names

Index of Names

Index of Names and Index of Musicals

Index of Musicals

The composer is mentioned with works of musical theater.

Index of Musicals

Index of Musicals

Index of Musicals and Picture Credits

Picture Credits